CORAL GABLES
Miami Riviera

AN ARCHITECTURAL GUIDE

by Aristides J. Millas and Ellen J. Uguccioni

This project has been financed in part with historic preservation grant assistance provided by the National Park Service, U.S. Department of the Interior, administered through the Bureau of Historic Preservation, Division of Historical Resources, Florida Department of State, assisted by the Historic Preservation Advisory Council. However, the contents and opinions do not necessarily reflect the views and opinions of the Department of the Interior or the Florida Department of State, nor does the mention of trade names or commercial products constitute endorsement or recommendation by the Department of the Interior or the Florida Department of State. This program receives Federal financial assistance for identification and protection of historic properties. Under Title VI of the Civil Rights Act of 1964, Section 504 of the Rehabilitation Act of 1973, and the Age Discrimination Act of 1975, as amended, the U.S. Department of the Interior prohibits discrimination on the basis of race, color, national origin, disability, or age in its federally assisted programs. If you believe you have been discriminated against in any program, activity, or facility as described above, or if you desire further information, please write to: Office of Equal Opportunity, National Park Service, 1849 C Street, NW, Washington, DC 20240.

Note: Unless otherwise noted all historical photos courtesy of the Florida State Archives. Contemporary photos in tours: Millas Collection.

Cover: rendering of Douglas Entrance by Bob Fink 1926
Inside covers: paintings by Denman Fink, poetry excerpts by George Merrick "The Tamiami Trail" and "Song of the Wind"
Book Design: Inkbyte Design
Printing: Fine Printing
Publisher: The Dade Heritage Trust
ISBN No. 0-9620565-1-0
Library of Congress Card Control Number 2003094285

DADE HERITAGE TRUST
190 S.E. 12th Terrace
Miami, Florida 33131
(305) 358-9572

TABLE OF CONTENTS

Advertisement for the sale of the first lots in Coral Gables, November 1921

5

ACKNOWLEDGEMENTS

The authors wish to acknowledge and thank the following individuals: the Honorable Donald D. Slesnick, Mayor of the City of Coral Gables, for his continued support of the project and his preface to this book; The Villagers, Inc., Dade County's oldest historic preservation organization, for their generous donation under President Victoria Belcher; Rebecca Roper Matkov, Executive Director of the Dade Heritage Trust; and the late Samuel D. LaRoue Jr., an impassioned avocational historian who gave much support, time and valuable assistance to the realization of this book. We are also indebted to the following: Fay Bernardo, who selflessly coordinated and produced the text of this publication despite her immense workload as Faculty Secretary to the University of Miami's School of Architecture; Dr. Sherry Piland, who offered considerable insight into the study of early city planning efforts; graduate student Carolina Moscoso for her invaluable assistance and University of Miami alumni Charles Stevens, Juan Cacciamani, and Cesar Mendoza. To the following individuals we offer our thanks for the many different levels of assistance without which this publication could not have been produced: Donna Lubin and Simone Chin of the City's Historic Preservation Department; Elizabeth Plater-Zyberk, Dean of the University of Miami School of Architecture; and faculty colleagues David Burnett, Jan Hochstim, Frank Martinez, Carie Penabad, and especially Andrea Gollin, Publications Manager at the Knight Program in Community Building. Our thanks also to computer lab technician Gary Jaggernauth; Peter Roman of Inkbyte Design; Steven Steele of Fine Printing; Leslie Sheffield of the Florida Bureau of Archives; the University of Miami Otto Richter Library (Archives and Special Collections); Habib Haddad at University of Miami Facilities Administration; the Historical Association of Southern Florida; Pauline Saliga, Executive Director of the Society of Architectural Historians; Mitchell Kaplan of Books & Books; Ron Gabor; Dr. Fred Nagle; Malinda Cleary; Robbie McNamara; Carol Millas; and Leah LaPlante.

Dedicated to the memory of Samuel D. LaRoue Jr.

PREFACE

THE CITY OF CORAL GABLES

The City Beautiful

OFFICE OF THE MAYOR

CITY HALL 405 BILTMORE WAY
CORAL GABLES, FLORIDA 33134

October 31, 2002

We are delighted to herald the publication of <u>Coral Gables: Miami Rivera – An Architectural Guide.</u> This much-anticipated book is a worthy addition to the rich collection of literature surrounding the somewhat mythical history of our community, locally known as the "City Beautiful".

Coral Gables is a community envisioned by a Congregational minister's son who attempted to breathe life into the prophet Ezekiel's vision of a walled and gated, palm-laden heavenly city on earth. On the secular side, he added some visual hints of 19th century romanticism. Despite land sale busts, hurricanes, and the Great Depression, the "Gables" has burst onto the twenty-first century architectural scene as a truly great example of the 1920's North American suburban village.

For over 75 years, those of us who have been entrusted with the governance of Coral Gables have labored untiringly to preserve (rather than alter) its unique character which combines serene residential neighborhoods with a vibrant, robust commercial district.

Following the lead of this guide book you will be introduced to intriguing Mediterranean vistas full of tropical gardens and architectural flights-of-fancy. Relax and allow the tours outlined within these pages to transport you to Washington Irving's "Alhambra", or, in reality, to George Merrick's "Miami Riviera".

Don Slesnick
Mayor

INTRODUCTION

The idea for this self guided tour book originated in the summer of 2000 when the authors as co-chairs were making preparations to host the 52nd Annual Meeting of the Society of Architectural Historians in the City of Coral Gables at the venerable and beautiful Biltmore Hotel. We had been planning tours to showcase the unique architecture and historic neighborhood communities of the greater Miami region including Coral Gables. Apart from a map distributed by the City, there was no pocket-sized publication that allowed visitors the opportunity to learn the history and tour the city's landmarks on their own. Initial support to produce such a tour guide was given by the Coral Gables Cultural Affairs Advisory Board, the "Villagers" Historic Preservation organization and the Dade Heritage Trust, which agreed to sponsor this educational publication when financial support was sought from the Florida Department of State Division of Historical Resources, for which we are very grateful.

Coral Gables is indeed very unique. It is unique in its sense of place, of which one becomes immediately aware when entering the city from almost any direction. Lush verdant landscaping abounds and romantic images are created everywhere by the historic architecture and the landscape. Coral Gables is first and foremost a "city of homes" as it has been characterized from its beginnings in the 1920s. It is a historical city that began as the "Master Suburb" and was incorporated as a city in less than four years from the sale of the first lots in November 1921. The city created by its founder George E. Merrick and his team was an artistic and poetic vision. Beautiful sketches and renderings accompanied every development phase and were published in promotional literature which was circulated nationwide to a winter-weary public.

It is the authors' intent to re-affirm that vision by including as many historic photos and illustrations as possible when explaining the chronological and remarkable development of the city collected during an on-going process of sponsored research since the mid 1980s. Tours in this book are principally organized by sectors of the city related to the founding concepts either spatially or by architectural themes. We hope to provide the reader with an interesting and memorable way of "looking at the city."

Aristides J. Millas and Ellen J. Uguccioni

PART I

CORAL GABLES: THE CITY INSPIRED

∞

As I gaze on their mystical splendor,
    From the palm-grove beside of the sea;
I glimpse of a land where the fancy may enter
    But never the spirit may be.
— GEORGE MERRICK

B etween 1911 and 1921, an aspiring poet named George E. Merrick began his lifelong affair with real estate. It was an inspired connection, as this man who created images with words could capture those poetic images and literally "cast them in stone." The City of Coral Gables was his greatest achievement.

The maturation of his ideas was a combination of his own inspiration coupled with a practical apprenticeship acquired while in the real estate industry. As a young man in his 20s, Merrick was involved in the sales of significant Miami subdivisions. In his own reflections, Merrick points to his study of other cities, such as Boston, Chicago, and Cleveland, as important precursors for his own master development. City planning in the USA had in fact made significant progress in the half-century before Merrick began his own plan. Many of those ideas would find expression in Coral Gables, a Miami suburb incorporated as a city in 1925, just four years after the first lots were sold.

Late 19th and Early 20th Century Development Trends

When the appellation "City Beautiful" is applied to Coral Gables, the term is used more as a description than as an historical reference to an important phase in city planning. Nevertheless, Coral Gables does merit a place in the history of urban development, and it is useful to briefly review the genesis of planning ideals in the United States, as it influenced Merrick's plan.

In the 19th century, life changed for the world when a rural agrarian economy gave way to the industrial age. The move away from the

Early sales office 1922 with George E. Merrick and Edward "Doc"
Dammer (foreground right)
Opposite page: Painting for poem "The Cloud Mountains of Florida," Denman Fink

family farm to the city frequently resulted in overcrowding and the destruction of the natural landscape. Epidemics, noise, and stench were some of the Dickensian consequences of this unplanned growth.

By the end of the century Americans were caught up in the need to refashion their cities in order to promote social, cultural, and economic harmony. Hundreds of civic improvement societies sprang up in a desire to systematically deal with the issues of transportation, utilities, sanitation, public health, and recreation. The City Beautiful movement was a result of those efforts.

Famed landscape architect Frederick Law Olmsted set the stage for this movement. During the years between 1857 and 1870, Olmsted developed his theories about the role of landscape in an urban setting. His successful integration of parks, and later his extensive use of a park and boulevard system, would become the mainstays of the City Beautiful movement.

The City Beautiful movement had its greatest impact on American city planning between 1900 and 1910. The World's Columbian Exposition of 1893, celebrating the discovery of America by Christopher Columbus, is generally considered the first large scale and readily comprehensible expression of City Beautiful ideals. The Exposition had an enormous impact on the dissemination of those ideals, even though their concrete expression occurred a few years later.

The key components in a City Beautiful scheme included the comprehensive planning of the whole, the creation of grand civic centers, the provision for tree-lined boulevards and substantial green spaces, and the creation of public sculpture and civic monuments. The movement recognized that artistic attention could be expressed in even the most fundamental of urban requirements, such as street signs and lampposts.

In 1897, members of the Arts and Crafts Society used the description in England. In the United States between 1898 and 1902 the "City Beautiful" characterization was used by the municipal art movement as a slogan to describe proposals that would enhance the physical qualities of a city. Charles Mulford Robinson, a highly influential city planner (at the time he was practicing, city planning had not yet been established as a formal discipline), popularized the use of the phrase. Between 1902 and 1904, he published a series of syndicated newspaper articles entitled "The City Beautiful."

Base of cast iron Coral Gables lampost

The principles of the City Beautiful movement, and particularly the emphasis on interconnecting parks and boulevards, were incorporated into a number of planning schemes throughout the country. Cities such as Kansas City, Missouri; Denver, Colorado; Seattle, Washington; Harrisburg, Pennsylvania (the first US city to adopt the slogan "City Beautiful" in its promotional campaign); and Orlando, Florida, which followed immediately in 1908, are considered excellent examples of the City Beautiful influence in the early 20th century.

The City Beautiful movement was not without its critics. Some derided its aesthetic influence and the extravagance of its cost, managing to discredit the movement. In its place came new ideas that emphasized efficiency and practicality. This new version in urban planning was known variously as the "City Scientific," the "City Practical," or the "City Efficient."

The City of Coral Gables was not the first planned city in the United States, nor was it constructed during the time when City Beautiful movement ideals were widely embraced. The City of Coral Gables has earned its reputation as an exceptional American city because of the completeness of its original concept and plan. It is a great city because of its early conception and execution and because of its inspired combination of pragmatism and poetry.

Because Merrick was starting with a "blank" canvas, he and his team of designers were free to adopt the best attributes of other cities, while avoiding the pitfalls of earlier examples. By combining the principles espoused by early planning leaders, Merrick created a city that can rightfully be called beautiful.

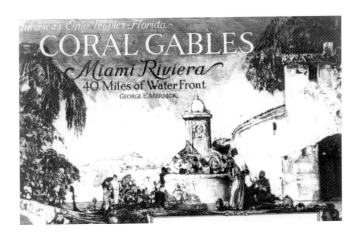

Coral Gables advertisement, c.1925

Not A City But A Suburb

When Merrick first began the sale of his new development he specifically referred to his creation as a "suburb." His land, after all, began as a thriving avocado and grapefruit plantation, and he looked to the City of Miami, some five miles to the east and incorporated in 1896, as the closest urban center.

In 1871 Frederick Law Olmsted defined a suburb as "...detached dwellings with a considerable share of urban convenience." Implied in that description is the desire for amenities associated with country living, which included limitless amounts of fresh air and an environment liberally laced with trees, green spaces, and water-courses. In 1923 Merrick published two promotional booklets, one entitled "Miami's Master Suburb" and the other "America's Finest Suburb." He stated:

> The whole great acreage is developed as a city would be as far as buildings go, but so placed that the whole country side becomes a wide, green and gracious city, and the city becomes a combination of park and garden, and country expanse.

The realization of suburbia for Merrick was in the provision of city conveniences while capitalizing on the sylvan qualities associated with country living.

The *sine qua non*, which insured the growth of suburbia, was the availability of land, combined with the availability of transportation. Together they allowed the base from which a community outside of the city could grow and the transportation necessary to bring

Coral Way in 1922

the community's residents back and forth to the city where they were employed. Architect Robert A. M. Stern reflects: "The suburb is...a state of mind based upon imagery and symbolism. Suburbia's curving roads and tended lawns, its houses with pitched roofs, shuttered windows, and colonial or otherwise elaborate doorways all speak of communities which value the tradition of the family, pride of ownership, and rural life."

The introduction of suburbs as an alternative to city dwelling can again be traced to the generation before Merrick. Olmsted and other early planners began the regulation of building standards, design controls, lot size, and building placement in their development of the new suburb. These controls existed long before formal zoning existed. Communal architectural styles were also introduced as part of these homogenous plans.

The 1854 suburb of Chestnut Hill, located within the boundaries of Philadelphia, serves as an interesting foil in our review of communities that may have had a direct impact on the creation of Coral Gables. Developers Henry Howard Houston and Dr. George Woodward (the heir to the original developer) were interested in earlier English experiments in semi-detached housing. Houston and Woodward employed renowned local architects to create an overall character to the suburb, where a consistent stylistic theme would dominate and come to characterize the place. In 1919 in a design for the "French Village" by architect Robert Rodes McGoodwin, Norman-styled gatehouses were introduced at the entrance to Chestnut Hill.

For one group of homes an English Cotswold style was used and local building materials employed. The homes were thus a product of their own locality, and the designs were harmonious and fitting with the rustic French styles already popular in the town.

The hallmark characteristics of Chestnut Hill are its use of indigenous building materials; the employment of accomplished architects; the use of gates as symbolic points of entry; and the seminal idea that individual houses can maintain their own identity, while still contributing to their collective character as an ensemble. Merrick was to employ these concepts to full advantage.

While strictly conjectural, one could easily believe that Chestnut Hill made a strong impact on one of the masterminds of Coral Gables, the architect Phineas Paist. Paist, who was to become Merrick's supervising architect, was born, raised, and educated in Philadelphia. The proximity of Chestnut Hill makes it more than likely that Paist would have been familiar with its community concepts.

In an article published in the *Jacksonville Times Union,* Merrick cites the 1916 development of Shaker Heights, just outside Cleveland, as closest to his own concepts of ideal development. Shaker Heights was a residential community of 10,000, begun by developers O.P. and M.J. Van Sweringen in 1916. Their development was strictly regulated as to architectural styles; building materials and even appropriate colors were dictated. The components of historic English and French architecture with their steep roof pitches, brick construction, and details, such as shutters, windows, doors, and chimneys were ideally suited to the climate and geography of this Ohio suburb. It was this adaptability of the building to its climate and place that so impressed Merrick. He reasoned that the environment was the predicator from which all development schemes must depend.

In his introduction to *The Anglo American Suburb,* Robert A. M. Stern tells us that the results of the industrialization of America caused increased prosperity and moral problems that damaged spiritual life. In his view, those repercussions helped fuel the increasingly popular growth of the American suburb. Certainly Merrick was aware of these issues, as his definition of the suburb addressed those very problems. In his brochure *Coral Gables Facts* published in January 1927, Merrick summarized the attributes of a great city:

> A well planned city, beautiful homes, widest range of scholastic activities, with the material, the communal, the municipal and the cultural phases of life fittingly rounded out by those religious organizations, so especially a part of the foundation of American life and outlook – the whole developing a highly conscious citizenship. That is Coral Gables.

Merrick's concern for quality of life, realized in both brick and mortar and in the cultural and educational opportunities he planned for his community, resulted in a suburb yet without equal.

The Team Approach

In order to realize his plans, Merrick surrounded himself with others whose combined expertise and vision could accomplish his goals. This commingling of disciplines recalls the ideals of the City Beautiful movement when the collaboration of architects, sculptors, engineers, and landscape architects insured the integration of beauty, utility, harmony, and continuity.

Even before the first lots were sold in November 1921, Merrick sought advice from his uncle, an artist who created vivid and picturesque images in two dimensions. The pictorial quality of the city is largely due to the efforts of Denman Fink (1881-1956). Fink had studied art in Pittsburgh, Boston, and New York, and had become a highly

successful illustrator. His images appeared in *Harpers*, *The Century*, *Hearst*, and *Scribner's* magazines. Fink was a member of the National Academy of Art and his work had been the subject of a number of exhibitions.

Fink, who was given the title "Art Director" or sometimes "Artist-in-Chief," looked to Merrick's design team for the translation of those images into three dimensions. The team of six architects who set the prototypical designs for Coral Gables from its inception was: H. George Fink (Merrick's cousin), Martin Luther Hampton, Walter De Garmo, Richard Kiehnel, Harold Hastings Mundy, and Lewis D. Brumm. Fink designed the majority of the early coral rock houses that line Coral Way. De Garmo came from a Beaux Arts tradition, but quickly grasped the defining characteristics of Mediterranean style, developing both residential and commercial designs. Martin L. Hampton had earlier worked with Addison Mizner in Palm Beach and was quite familiar with adaptations of Spanish architecture. Richard Kiehnel had just completed his inspired work in the design for the John Bindley mansion in Coconut Grove, a masterpiece of Mediterranean design. Both Brumm and Mundy were more than proficient in creating the thematic architecture employed for Coral Gables.

After Coral Gables' initial development, Merrick hired the man who would make a permanent impact on the process for design approval in the city. Phineas Paist, originally from Philadelphia, had come to the Miami area in 1916 at the request of Paul Chalfin who was designing the magnificent Italianate Villa Vizcaya for James Deering.

Above: Coral Gables Administration Building, October 1925 (demolished)

Paist was named associate architect on the Vizcaya project, and he later designed a villa in South Dade for Deering's brother Charles that was completed in 1922. In the creation of Coral Gables, Paist first held the title "Supervisor of Color" and was later named "Supervising Architect" for the Coral Gables Corporation. It was Paist who set up the review process that required a high standard of design for all buildings constructed within the city. Today that same review process is conducted through an appointed panel called the "Board of Architects."

Two other critical ingredients in the creation of this ideal city were civil engineering and landscape architecture. Frank M. Button (1860–1938), Merrick's landscape architect, was educated in Vermont, and later employed briefly as an assistant engineer for the World's Columbian Exposition (1893). While in Chicago, Button served as the landscape architect for a series of private estates in the Lake Forest suburb, and designed the extension to Lincoln Park. Civil Engineer W. C. Bliss, after arriving in Miami, opened a partnership (Bailey, Bliss and Watson) and was fully responsible for the engineering of Merrick's new development.

The Symbiotic Relationship Of Architecture & Environment

Always it seemed to me that there should be the same class of houses and surroundings which were along the shores of the Mediterranean. Geographically and climatically, South Florida is identified with Spain, North Africa, and all that lies between them and the South Sea Islands. — George Edgar Merrick, 1925

Though he himself had never traveled to the places he refers, Merrick instinctively seemed to understand the harmony of Mediterranean architecture in his vision for Coral Gables. There is an abundance of quotes from the Merrick team concerning their architectural vision for the city. The language is colorful, romantic, and infinitely beautiful:

Sunsets and moonlights are by them made household ornaments which these homes are built to include. Orange blossoms and thrumburgia vines and jasmines and night blooming cereus are here made friends of the household, along with the ecstatic ripples of the mocking bird's song in moonlight and the green-gold blur of hummingbird's wings.

Landscape and the naturally occurring beauty of the place were as critical as the built environment in creating the perfect suburb. In an advertisement published in February 1926, the promoters of the City of Coral Gables emphasized that the magnificent avenues and plazas were designed to emphasize the spectacular beauty of the sky and sea, of brilliant tropical shrubbery, of stately pines and dramatic coconut palms.

In the beginning the raw landscape of Coral Gables was principally pineland, a vast dense tropical hammock laden with scrub palmetto. This landscape was enhanced by the planting of fully grown flowering shrubs and trees, many of them imported from the nearby Florida Keys. By October 1924, over 50,000 trees, shrubs and flowering plants had been installed and another 40,000 were being propagated in nurseries.

The vocabulary of design in Coral Gables defies rigorous stylistic classification, leading to frustration on the part of some who wish there to be no ambiguity. In the least descriptive fashion, the Coral Gables Corporation's Warranty Deed puts it thusly: "All buildings shall be constructed of Spanish, Venetian, Moorish, Italian, or other similarly harmonious types of architecture."

Above: Gateway to Coral Gables (imagined), painting by Denman Fink, 1922
Center: The groves of Coral Gables, looking southeast from first water tower, July 1922

The most commonly used and accepted term to describe the architectural style is Mediterranean Revival. The buildings depend on fine construction, extensive wall mass with beautifully proportioned details, and not on superficial detail for their overall effect. Walls were of tinted stucco, frequently rough textured so that they caught changing light and shadow. Broken planes were created through the use of curves, the combination of one and two story elements, and the use of differing roof pitches. For example, a series of arched windows could break the wall mass, and in the front porches, a triple arched veranda might provide an elegant entry. While superficial ornament was avoided, detail abounded everywhere. Ventilator holes were grouped for decorative effect, ironwork graced balconies and windows, chimneys possessed raised stucco banding, and frequently, parapets were shaped adding curved lines to the otherwise horizontal planes.

Interior plans were adapted to take maximum advantage of the hospitable climate. Patios, verandahs, courtyards, wide living rooms, and sleeping porches, were all common "indoor-outdoor" amenities, for it was nature itself in all its bountiful sub-tropical glory that became one of the basic building blocks of the architectural formula.

The tours in the chapters that follow illustrate the permeating themes of this inspired planning. Their organization is at times reflective of the city's chronological development, but more often is based upon key concepts that together result in a harmonious and inspired whole.

— Ellen J. Uguccioni

Opposite page top: Post at Ponce de Leon Plaza, June 1925
Above: Residence at 1104 Malaga Ave, May 1926
Above: Residence at 2715 Alhambra Circle, Oct. 1926

PART II

CORAL GABLES
THE CHRONOLOGICAL
DEVELOPMENT

∞

C oral Gables was documented in the National Park Service Historic American Building Survey (HABS) as "An Historic New Town" in 1971. That document explains that the city is a significant historic area for several reasons. It is unique in America in the completeness of its original concept and plan as a suburban community at a time when real estate "developments" were no more than a gridiron of streets marked by entrance posts. In addition to planning for every conceivable activity that would be the foundation for a community, the concept was unique, at the time, for the amount of land provided as open spaces for recreation areas and a system of wide boulevards at a time of rapidly rising land values in the "boom" era 1920's. Landscaping and a pre-determined architectural character were integral to the plan from its inception as a picturesque vision. It is unique also in that the concept and its major implementation were the results of a collaboration between a poet (turned real estate developer), George E. Merrick, and an artist, his uncle, Denman Fink, and several gifted local architects led by his cousin H. George Fink.

Beginnings

Coral Gables began humbly in 1893 when William H. Gregory began homesteading 160 acres of virgin timberland whose southern boundary was the existing Coral Way. When he sold the property in July 1899 for $1,100 to the Reverend Solomon G. Merrick, a Congregational minister from Duxbury, Massachusetts, it contained, among other improvements, a small frame house and 300 tropical fruit plants on 25 acres. The land eventually became the Coral Gables Plantation, so named for the coral rock addition designed in 1905 by Althea Fink Merrick, his wife. The house today is the present "Coral Gables Merrick House" and functions as a museum and archives at 907 Coral Way.

Above: The Merrick Homestead, 1899
Opposite page: Comprehensive bird's eye map, Nov. 1925

George Merrick, the eldest son, in a 1925 interview (*Jacksonville Times Union*, Jan. 28, 1925), relates that before his death in 1911, his father expressed the idea of subdividing the property and selling five-acre tracts to other retired ministers and professionals. The idea of Coral Gables as a subdivision thus originated with the Reverend Merrick. However, in the interview George Merrick continued that he did not like his father's idea. Instead, he "dreamed of someday seeing here 1000 homes which would make my 'castles in Spain a reality.'" He was referring to his own earliest dreams, convinced that South Florida was "geographically and climatically identical with Spain, North Africa and the South Seas."

Young Merrick's education at New York Law School was interrupted by his father's death, when he returned to Florida to manage the family plantation. By 1916 he had married and been appointed a County Commissioner. Merrick opened a real estate office and by selling subdivisions elsewhere realized a profit which he used to buy lands adjacent to the plantation. His holdings increased from the original 160 acres to 3000 acres when the first lots were sold in Coral Gables in 1921. Maps included here illustrate the plantation boundaries of 560 acres as determined from Dade County maps in 1915 (see Map 2 on page 27).

The first double-page advertisement of Coral Gables appeared in a Miami newspaper dated November 14, 1921. George Merrick himself wrote "the building of Coral Gables...a wonderful monument to the achievement of worthwhile perseverance in the creation of beauty and the bringing true of dreams." Merrick later expressed his ideal of beauty, combined with the profit motive, when he said, "Beauty can be made to pay."

Although practically every promotional brochure and booklet published by Merrick appealed strongly to the orderly visual and physical amenities awaiting residents of Coral Gables, they stressed at the same time the investment possibilities of this new "residential community."

Miami Sales Office, E. Flagler St., 1922

The Florida "boom" was just beginning to attract nationwide attention. Coral Gables was to become the largest single unit of the South Florida land boom of 1921–26 with approximately $150 million in real estate sales and $100 million in direct expenditures (*Miami Millions*). Ambitions and projections were extremely high. The City of Miami Beach had already been developed from a mangrove swamp to become incorporated in 1915 and was later linked by trolley to downtown Miami with the opening of the County Causeway in 1920. Miami was in various stages of rapid growth expanding northward, westward, and southward beyond the original two square mile plan of Henry Flagler and Julia Tuttle (1896).

The Chronology of Development

The planning of Coral Gables went far beyond the then-current concepts of subdivisions containing mere housing laid out within a gridiron pattern of streets. Rather, the designers and engineers would think in terms of what a complete suburban community would require (the "Master Suburb"). At this point, Frank M. Button, a landscape architect from Chicago, must be credited as the actual planner of the city. In a letter to George E. Merrick on April 18, 1921, he offered "to make plans for the subdivision known as Coral Gables...comprising about 1200 acres, on a basis of $1.00 per acre." This letter was signed "Approved" by George E. Merrick.

A map of Coral Gables dated October 1921 by W. C. Bliss, civil engineer, and Frank Button is the most reliable source for the original plan of 1200 acres which indicate the first "Section A." A later comprehensive map by Bliss (1924) (Map 1) would designate all sections, blocks, and lots, except for the area south of the "proposed Biltmore Golf Course" which was titled "Under Development." This map, together with historic photographs included in this publication, illustrates not only the essentials of the plan but also the amazing speed with which it was being implemented. Entrances, plazas, and important buildings are also noted on the 1924 map. The plan for the first 1200 acres established Coral Way as the major east-west axis and Granada Boulevard as the major north-south axis. The 1921 map illustrates this boulevard with an extension northward to the Tamiami Trail (S.W. 8th Street today) where the first Granada entrance would be constructed. Most of the plazas would be located at major automobile intersections along these two axes, Coral Way and Granada Boulevard. The intersections would be spatially defined with perimeter walls, lampposts, fountains, pergolas, and colorful landscaping.

Granada Sec.

S. E. Sec C

GRANADA

Sec. A

GOLF LAND COUNTRY CLUB GOLF COURSE

College for Young Women of the Sisters of St. Joseph

Country Club Sec.
Part 1

NEW CLUB HOUSE

18 HOLE GOLF COURSE

UNDER DEVELOPMENT

DIXIE HIGHWAY

COUNTRY CLUB PRADO

ALHAMBRA

GRANADA BOULEVARD

CONGREGATION CHURCH

VENETIAN POOL

BIRD ROAD

ALHAMBRA CIRCLE

GREENWAY DRIVE

SOUTH GREENWAY DRIVE

SOROLLA AVENUE

OBISPO AVENUE

ASTURIA AVENUE

CASTILE AVENUE

VALENCIA AVENUE

ALMERIA AVENUE

CATALONIA AVENUE

ANASTASIA

PLAZA AUGUSTINE CORAL

PLAZA PONCE DE LEON CORAL

PLAZA COLUMBIA

PLAZA SALVADOR

PLAZA DE SOTO

PLAZA GRANADA

SAN MARCO AVENUE

SANTA CRUZ

SAN BENITO

MALAGA

VENETIA

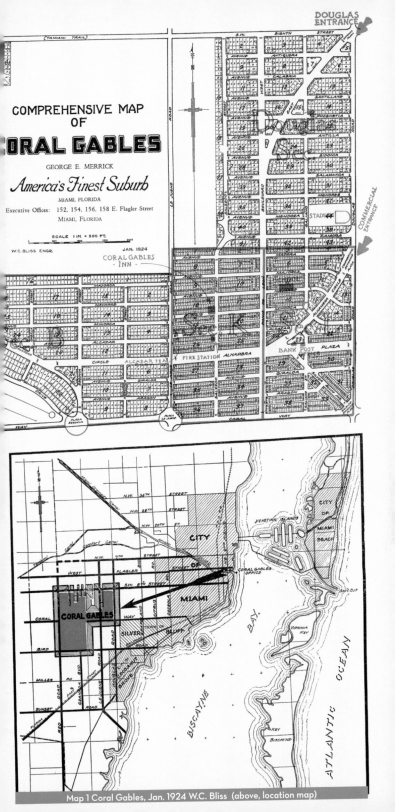

Map 1 Coral Gables, Jan. 1924 W.C. Bliss (above, location map)

On November 17, 1921 when the first lots were sold, the *Miami Herald* reproduced the following article by Frank M. Button:

> On all the principal boulevards at Coral Gables have been laid out delightful parks, plazas and rest spots, one-half to five acres in area, that break the vistas of the avenues and provide the most charming possibilities for landscape work of the most effective kind... Whenever possible fruit trees in parkways between sidewalks and streets have been preserved, and for miles the visitor to Coral Gables walks through veritable bowers laden with delectable fruit.
>
> The two golf courses...are bordered with native palms, pines, live oaks, wild figs, ferns, and other tropical shrubbery that delight the nature lover and make ideal surroundings for golf...The nine-hole course is well under way now, and is 2,900 yards in length, with a 500-yard hole, which will be a test for even the par golfer. The 18-hole course will have three holes of over 500 yards, and the entire course will be 5,574 yards, with good fairways, grass greens and traps and hazards of the most modern kind.
>
> Large plots have been set aside in prominent locations for churches, schools, library and other community centers...Winding boulevards encircle the entire tract, diagonal streets make every part accessible...Plantings of cocoanut, rubber, royal poinciana, grevilla, pithecolobium and bamboo trees, and shrubbery such as acalypha, hibiscus, oleander and jasmine, with alamanda, bougainvillea and many other varieties of vines, Coral Gables will present a home site development unsurpassed for ideal living conditions.

Included in this publication are two new maps of Coral Gables compiled from the Sanborn Map company for the years 1921 (Map 2) when the first lots were sold and June 1924 (Map 3) showing the footprint of every building constructed to that date. A comparison of the two maps clearly reveals the extent and rapidity with which Coral Gables was being developed, the facts of which were continually published in the "Coral Gables Miami Riviera" promotional publication. In the 1923 pamphlet, under the paragraph entitled "Hundreds of Distinctive Homes" Merrick writes "Coral Gables is first and last a distinctive residential suburb...The building of three hundred homes was an important feature of last year's great Development Program." It is from this map that the authors are able to determine the locations of the earliest homes from the coral rock houses along Coral Way to the

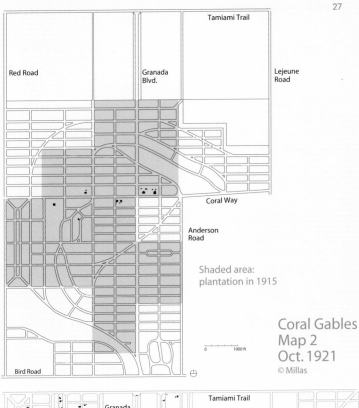

Shaded area:
plantation in 1915

Coral Gables
Map 2
Oct. 1921
© Millas

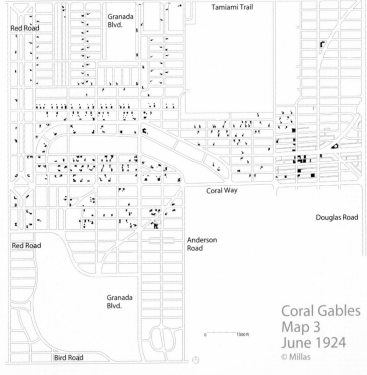

Coral Gables
Map 3
June 1924
© Millas

north-south streets connecting to the Tamiami Trail (S.W. 8th Street today), and in particular Obispo Ave., which had its own promotional brochure promoting the 33 houses which were constructed and sold in only three months. These were speculative homes skillfully crafted by the original Coral Gables architects in which no two were alike. A plan and elevation of "Cottage No. 8" by Walter DeGarmo, the first registered architect in South Florida, is included in this publication. This house still exists on Obispo Avenue as do many

others of the original Coral Gables homes.

Also included are original maps indicating the three stages of the growth of Coral Gables from November 1921 through December 1925 (Maps 4, 5, & 6) when the Biscayne Section was announced, which would be the third stage of development. The second stage of growth was the Riviera Section which was entitled "The Riviera Section and the University of Miami," which was a critically important dimension in Merrick's vision. He planned to have the University as the centerpiece his newly incorporated city. The Riviera Section announcement states that "The area of this portion of Coral Gables is approximately two thousand acres and with the older sections of Coral Gables on the north covering about three thousand acres and the great Cocoplum Section [later to be called Biscayne] of Coral Gables on the south, which borders the waters of Biscayne Bay with a shore

Above: View north, Columbus Boulevard from church tower showing first water tower, c. 1924
Center: Elevation, Cottage No. 8, 1028 Obispo Avenue (courtesy F. Martinez)

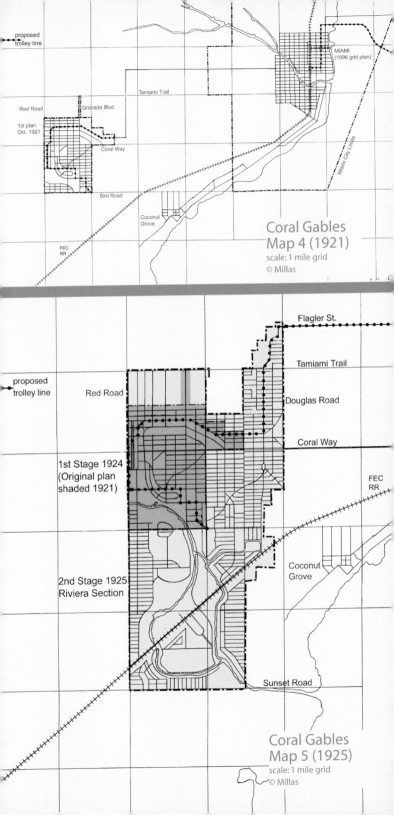

proposed
trolley line

Tamiami Trail

MIAMI
(1896 grid plan)

Red Road

Granada Blvd.

1st plan
Oct. 1921

Coral Way

Miami City Limits

Bird Road

Coconut
Grove

**Coral Gables
Map 4 (1921)**
scale: 1 mile grid
© Millas

FEC
RR

Flagler St.

proposed
trolley line

Red Road

Tamiami Trail

Douglas Road

Coral Way

FEC
RR

1st Stage 1924
(Original plan
shaded 1921)

2nd Stage 1925
Riviera Section

Coconut
Grove

Sunset Road

**Coral Gables
Map 5 (1925)**
scale: 1 mile grid
© Millas

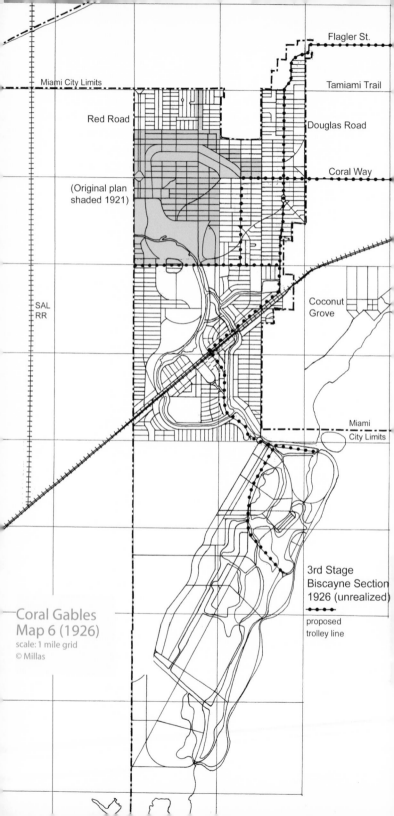

Flagler St.

Miami City Limits

Tamiami Trail

Red Road

Douglas Road

Coral Way

(Original plan
shaded 1921)

SAL
RR

Coconut
Grove

Miami
City Limits

3rd Stage
Biscayne Section
1926 (unrealized)

•–•–•–•

proposed
trolley line

Coral Gables
Map 6 (1926)
scale: 1 mile grid
© Millas

line seven miles and which embraces about five thousand acres, makes up the entire territory included in the City of Coral Gables approximately a total of ten thousand acres, or about sixteen square miles." Coral Gables, which began as a small plantation of 160 acres five miles west of Miami, finally reached the shores of Biscayne Bay as an incorporated city of 16 square miles. This would coincide with the peak of the Florida land boom prior to the devastating hurricane which hit the Miami region in September 1926 and contributed significantly to the collapse of the real estate market and eventually the young city's bankruptcy proceedings.

Included in this publication is a map from the Financial and Administrative Survey of the City of Coral Gables by the Municipal Consultant Service of the National Municipal League which illustrates the city's greatest extension of expansion (1934) along with recommendations to achieve financial solvency (Map 7). The report states: "Coral Gables was the center of the most spectacular real estate promotion in the history of our country. The city was planned on a scale adequate for a population of more than a quarter of a million. In 1930, it actually had a population of 5697 in an area of 16.5 square miles." The report continues: "The attempt to spread its activities over such a wide area brought ruin to the once great Coral Gables Corporation and led that corporation to contrive the transfer of some of its most burdensome responsibilities to the city government." The map divides the city into four districts with District No. 1 corresponding closely with the original comprehensive plan for the city (1924) where 5/6 of the population resides; District No. 2 corresponds with the Riviera section south of Bird Road and north of Sunset Drive and was "almost wholly vacant"; District No. 3

was the former "Central Miami" development west of Red Road and described as "uninhabited everglades land"; District No. 4 corresponds with the Biscayne section and Key Biscayne and did contain four large estates in 1934.

It would take the City of Coral Gables until August 1, 1961 to pay the final principal dividend on its debt incurred from the Florida boom of the 1920s when in 1930 the city defaulted on $8,750,000 in bonds.

Entrance posts to Central Miami (later Coral Gables) at the waterway on Red Road, 1925. Design attributed to Denman Fink.

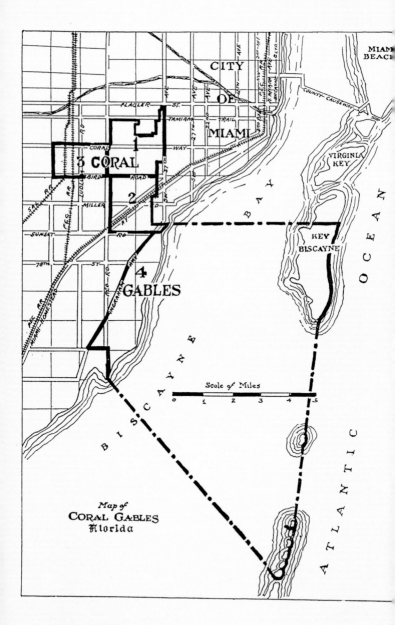

Coral Gables
Map 7 (1934)

The Planning Components

The documentation of Coral Gables in the Historic American Building Survey by the late Professor Woodrow Wilkins describes the new town with the following planning components in order to demonstrate the thoroughness which Merrick and his team would give to the "Master Suburb" they were envisioning. They are summarized here.

The Entrances and Plazas: Two major spatial concepts, the entrances and the plazas, can be attributed to Merrick's uncle, Denman Fink. Their philosophy is best expressed by Denman Fink on November 19, 1921 when he wrote: "The entrances, themselves, will hold out the promise of beauty and repose within...they will stand constantly with a wide open armed welcome to the passer-by." He continues: "it is our purpose to make these open spaces at the junction of streets and avenues, plazas in the real sense...scaled to harmonize with their surroundings." These entrances and plazas set the major theme of spaciousness and scale in Coral Gables.

A grand total of seven entrance gateways were planned. By the end of 1924, the Commercial and Granada entrances had been completed and the Country Club Prado entrance was under construction. Each entrance was conceived as a different expression. The concept culminates in the Douglas Entrance which was not opened until 1927, never to be completed according to the original design sketches. The Gladeside, Bayside, and Coconut Grove entrances were never constructed in the original development.

A 1923 promotional brochure states that six of the eight plazas indicated in the Bliss 1924 map were completed. These were Ponce de Leon Plaza at Coral Way and Granada Boulevard, Columbus Plaza at Coral Way and Columbus Boulevard, Balboa Plaza, Granada Plaza, LeJeune Plaza, and Segovia Plaza.

Granada Entrance imagined, painting by Denman Fink, 1922

Boulevards and Avenues: The spaciousness planned and achieved in Coral Gables is continued in the major arterial streets. By 1925 there were 100 miles of modern streets. This included Alhambra Circle, the longest, which is 120 feet wide, with a parkway in the center for its entire length as it winds diagonally from the commercial entrance on Douglas Road down to where it meets Campo Sano at the University of Miami in the southwest; Alhambra Plaza, 140 feet wide, is a short street in the business district which connects to Alhambra Circle at the western end; Coral Way is the main east-west avenue, varying in width from 120 feet to 70 feet, incorporating the famous "Miracle Mile," the main shopping street today, so renamed in 1944; Granada Boulevard, 100 feet wide, with a parkway on each side as the main north-south artery serving the residential section, beginning at the Granada Entrance on Tamiami Trail (Southwest 8th Street) on the north; Country Club Prado is the most

spacious boulevard, one and one-half miles long, 200 feet wide, with a center parkway, beginning at the colonnaded Prado Entrance on the Tamiami Trail, and running parallel to Red Road. Unlike Miami, in Coral Gables "avenues" run in an east-west direction and "streets" in a north-south direction.

Landscaping: In *Florida Living Magazine*, *Miami News*, February 4, 1962, Mrs. George E. Merrick is quoted, "His original plan was for the Gables to be a botanical garden with flowering trees at all times." Thus, landscaping was an essential feature of the plan. *The Miami Riviera, Coral Gables, Progress Edition*, November 12, 1926 reports, "The landscaping policy of Coral Gables is written into the cornerstone of the city by George E. Merrick as a fundamental principle...[it] has never been allowed to falter or to halt." The article further reports that the landscape department was headed by Frank M. Button, directing 130 landscape workers and two plant nurseries.

View from water tower at Alhambra Circle looking east, 1925

Waterways: The concept of open spaces in the city plan was continued in the development of the waterways and canals. They were being dredged eastward in 1925 and would serve the practical purpose of affording access to Biscayne Bay and the Atlantic Ocean. The seven miles of frontage on Biscayne Bay, acquired in the spring of 1925 by the Coral Gables Company, together with the waterfront of Key Biscayne, acquired prior to 1926, allowed Merrick to advertise "40 miles of waterfront." Key Biscayne is shown as part of Coral Gables in a second 1924 map but would later be returned to an unincorporated status.

Recreational Space: Vast amounts of land were dedicated in the original plan for recreational activities and in the majority of cases they were carried out. There were small parks, bridle paths, tennis courts, athletic fields, and the famous Venetian pool, carved out of a rock quarry used to furnish stone for the early constructions. The major open spaces were created by the golf courses. The first of these, the Granada Golf and Country Club, was completed in 1922.

Top: Coral Gables waterway dredging, looking east from Red Road, March 1924
Above: Coral Gables waterway with Miami Biltmore Hotel, 1926

Just five blocks south of the Granada course begins a vast sweep of space southward, defined on the north by the Biltmore Country Club with two 18-hole golf courses. It was completed in 1925, the same year that the Miami-Biltmore Hotel was under construction. The space then flows southward across Bird Road to the Riviera Country Club which bounded the proposed campus for the University of Miami. Also planned but never built was the Mahi Shrine and Golf Course south of Hardee Road.

The recreational potential of the waterfront, particularly on Biscayne Bay, was not ignored. The major seaside recreational space under construction at the same time as the Biltmore Hotel was Tahiti Beach, which was opened in February 1926. It was a complete Samoan village including community house, a chief's house, and one hundred individual huts, which were blown away in the hurricane of 1926.

Educational, Spiritual, and Cultural Planning: By 1923 the large new grammar school, which is still in use (Coral Gables Elementary), had been completed, and in 1924 the College for Young Women of the Sisters of St. Joseph was opened (now St. Teresa School). In the same year the Coral Gables Military Academy was announced.

Although construction of the University of Miami was not announced until May 1925, the idea for a university appeared very early in the planning. *The Miami Riviera,* January 13, 1928 quotes an advertisement dated December 18, 1921, "Chief among the ambitious projects…. Is the establishment of a university in Coral Gables." Merrick not only donated the site for the present University of Miami, but also made a gift of $5,000,000 to its endowment fund. Sketches for the proposed campus were published in *The Miami Herald,* June 3, 1925.

Above: Gondolas at Tahiti Beach, 1925

By November 1926 there were nine public and private schools in the city including the University High School and the University of Miami, which, because of the September 1926 hurricane, opened in the Anastasia Building on October 15, 1926.

The spiritual needs of the community were recognized very early in the development of Coral Gables. The cornerstone of the Congregational Church, the first church in Coral Gables, was laid in 1924. Merrick donated the land. Designed by Richard Kiehnel, it stands today opposite the Biltmore Hotel. In 1925 Merrick also donated land for the Roman Catholic Church of the Little Flower which opened in 1927.

Probably the most important provision in the plan for Coral Gables was the 7,500 seat coliseum which would serve the City of Miami as well as a major center for concerts, opera, and lectures. The announcement, complete with sketches, of this important building on Douglas Road appeared in the *Miami Riviera* September 1925. It was designed by A. Ten Ecyk Brown and August Geiger in a neo-classical style and dedicated on November 8, 1927. It has been demolished and a new housing project now takes its place. It is interesting to note in the Bliss map of January 1924 (pages 24–25) that general site area was originally intended for a stadium. A library was eventually established in the Cathedral Room of the Douglas Entrance nearby after it opened in 1927 and the commercial area contained two movie theaters. Civic clubs which enriched the community in many ways included the Coral Gables Woman's Club, the Cocoplum Woman's Club, a Garden Club, an American Legion Post, and the Kiwanis Club.

Above: St. Joseph's School for Girls, Walter De Garmo, Architect, Oct. 1926

Health Facilities: Health facilities were also recognized as important to the welfare of the community. In August 1925 Doctor H. M. Tallman announced plans for a clinic and hospital in the crafts section. Sketches by the architect, Phineas E. Paist, appeared in the *Miami Herald* July 27, 1925. It was located at Douglas Road and Coconut Boulevard and was in operation on June 14, 1926.

Hotels: With his faith in Florida as a winter resort it appears that Merrick placed hotel accommodations as a high priority in the development of the city. By 1925, four years after its beginning, Coral Gables boasted seven excellent hotels. Listed in the brochure *Coral Gables, Miami Riviera* (1925), by the Coral Gables Corporation, are the following hotels: The San Sebastian (exclusively for Coral Gables employees), the Lido Seville, the Anastasia (which housed the first classes of the University of Miami), the Coral Gables Inn, the Cla-Reina, the Antilla, and the Casa Loma. The Miami-Biltmore was under construction to open in grand style on January 15, 1926. A tentative comprehensive map of the Biscayne Bay section from 1925 indicates the proposed and probable location at Tahiti Beach for the "greatest" hotel of the Biltmore chain to contain more than 1,000 rooms. This concept was never realized.

A more ambitious, yet also unrealized dream was the Towers announced for the Riviera section in 1926. Patterned after the Kellogg Sanitarium in Battle Creek, Michigan, it was to be a hotel-like mega structure 688 feet in one direction and 588 feet in the other direction, with 1040 rooms. The announcement states "...that it would supply every human need for health and happiness...within the house and grounds of one magnificent hotel."

Above: Antilla Hotel at 1111 Ponce de Leon Boulevard, Oct. 1926 (demolished)

The Commercial District: In the 1921 map of Coral Gables the first business section was named Plaza Augustine and located between Coral Way and Anastasia Avenue and Red Road and Alhambra Circle. The area is described as a notably attractive parked boulevard with rest seats to make it delightful while shopping. The map also designates a library, a school, and buildings for other public uses. The Casa Loma Hotel was constructed nearby on the highest elevation in Coral Gables immediately west of the present day Biltmore Hotel. Aspirations for the growth of Miami were very great at this time, and for many years following the area to the west of Red Road was called "Central Miami" and at one time was even annexed by the City of Coral Gables. This may explain why the business district was originally planned to the west.

Shortly after the first lots were sold and Merrick's land holdings had increased to 3,000 acres, plans were extended eastward to Douglas Road to include the present day Commercial Center on sections K and L. A 1923 sales brochure describes the business section as lying on the eastern side of the property between LeJeune Road and Douglas Road. Its southern boundary is Coral Way, now being extended on the east to Brickell Avenue (in downtown Miami).

At this time, the new Commercial Entrance and gateway to the business section was constructed on Douglas Road at the junction of Alhambra Circle and described as being even more impressive than the Granada Entrance. Alhambra Circle was considered to be the principal boulevard of the business section which continues westward to encircle the entire suburb. Analysis of platting maps reveals that as Alhambra Circle meets Alhambra Plaza from the Commercial Entrance, it forms a direct axial relationship with the City Hall site

Above: Aerial view of Business District, Ponce de Leon Boulevard and Coral Way westward to LeJeune Plaza and city hall site, March 1926

and the Biltmore Hotel. The Douglas Entrance is also aligned on axis with the Biltmore Hotel site. George Merrick stated that the business section should be developed to the same high standards obtained in all of its fine residential sections – broad, spacious, and "parked" (landscaped) streets, boulevards, and avenues were envisioned in order to achieve beauty and distinction. He also said that the business section, while it is the only part of the property in which business buildings may be erected, is not restricted exclusively to commercial structures, as provisions were made for residential buildings. Thus Mr. Merrick and his planners envisioned a mixed-use concept for the business section.

An important feature of the business section was the creation, before 1923, of the arcaded shops of Coral Gables on Alhambra Circle and Lejeune Road. Promotional brochures extolled the virtues of shopping in modern Coral Gables "arcades" because one can wander from one fascinating shop to another regardless of the elements.

The opening of the Crafts Section south of the business section was announced in a promotional brochure dated October 1924 and illustrated with sketches by Phineas E. Paist. The crafts section had as its northern boundary Coral Way and its southern boundary was the midblock below San Sebastian Avenue. It contained two diagonal axis boulevards: Coconut Grove Drive which was aligned with the city hall site and the center of the Coconut Grove business district and Anastasia Avenue, which was later to become University Drive. The brochure is entitled "A New and Interesting Coral Gables Development Feature Offering Wonderful Opportunities for Profitable Development." The appeal was obviously to investors in the future of Coral Gables. The purpose was to foster craft industries which would not only serve the needs of

Above: Arcaded Shops of Coral Gables, LeJeune Road at Alhambra Circle, Walter De Garmo Architect, Aug. 1923 (demolished)

Coral Gables but would also serve a market throughout the entire country. The focal point of the crafts section was to have been the Exposition Center located in the present day Ponce Circle to display the wares created in the various shops.

In late August 1925 Merrick purchased the LeJeune plantation in order to plat the Biltmore section that was described as "a New Fifth Avenue Business District." This section ran from Coral Way to Altamari Avenue in the south and from Anderson Road to LeJeune Road in the east, and also offered rapid transit apartment sites. The section featured Biltmore Way as the connecting boulevard to the Miami-Biltmore Hotel which would be traversed by the rapid transit railway line to Segovia Avenue. Careful and wise building restrictions were equally applied to all the business sections which were advertised in promotional brochures entitled "Harmony in Business and Architecture." All buildings were prescribed to be of the similarly harmonious types of Mediterranean architecture and subject always to the approval of the supervising architect of Coral Gables.

The commercial success of the city is attested to by December 31, 1926 statistics when there were 601 licenses issued for 107 distinct lines of business. The 1927-28 *Coral Gables Pictorial Guide (and Classified Guide)* by A. B. Willis and Co. fully portrays the realization of these plans for the business sections of Coral Gables.

Communication and Transportation: Visualizing Coral Gables at first as a commuter suburb, "The Master Suburb" for Miami, it appears that Merrick realized the need for public transportation and planned accordingly. The 1924 map by Bliss indicates both

Coral Gables Trolley with William Jennings Bryan and George E. Merrick on left, 1925

streetcar and rapid transit routes. In 1925 trolley service had been instituted between Miami and Coral Gables out West Flagler Street and south along Ponce de Leon Boulevard. The rapid transit, an "express trolley," was not in operation, however, until May 10, 1926, advertising a 10-cent fare and a 20-minute ride to Miami along Coral Way. A local system of deluxe buses fed to and from the rapid transit line to Miami.

The Florida East Coast Railway Station was planned but never executed opposite the University of Miami. An announcement in 1925 stated that it would be the largest railway station south of Jacksonville for the railway company. In 1925 it was also announced that the Seaboard Airline Railroad would extend its lines from West Palm Beach to Miami with the construction of a station depot on Flagler Street near the Coral Gables entrance. The station was built at Coral Way and 72nd Avenue.

Building Restrictions: Thus it appears that George E. Merrick and Denman Fink had planned a total community in 1921 which would furnish its residents with amenities and luxuries not to be found in other real estate developments of its time. They later chose the definition of "city-region" for the new idea of Coral Gables as American's finest suburb because "it is a place developed to the highest degree for people to live in, more or less as a city is. So when we combine the idea of 'region' which means country, and 'city.' which is where men live, we got a better thing by calling it a 'city-region.' " (*Coral Gables: America's Finest Suburb, 1927*). More than any other previously planned community, however, there was an ingredient which was perhaps unique for the scale of the plan. This was what

Above: *Proposed Railroad Station by Schultze and Weaver Architects (unrealized), Oct. 1924*

amounted to complete control of the architecture from structural strength to architectural character. The latter had been pre-determined at the outset of the plan to assure Merrick's ideals of a harmonious cityscape and to guarantee value for investors.

The exacting requirements for construction were not tested and proven until the great hurricane which struck the area on September 17, 1926. Building failures in Coral Gables were minimal relative to other buildings in the area. All buildings had to measure up to these requirements which were set by Merrick's Board of Architects, headed by Phineas E. Paist. Thus, from the general city plan to the specific architectural detail, Merrick was able to exert a personal control on the quality and character of his suburb. Evidently, many persons had faith in his idea and his ideals. In 1925 building permits amounting to $25,890,515 were issued. By November 1926 there were 2,792 private homes and apartments accommodating 2,153 families and six fine hotels including the Miami Biltmore.

Coral Gables was a successful, completely planned city to its people. Matlack Price in *Arts and Decoration,* January 1925 aptly assessed the results when he stated "wrong start was eliminated by carefully zoning the plan and putting various restrictions on different areas."

Municipal Incorporation, April 1925: With the momentum of the Florida boom operating to Merrick's advantage, it was inevitable that Coral Gables would soon outgrow its designation as Miami's suburb and succumb to full-fledged incorporation. By 1925, it was in fact a "new town" despite the fact that it was under the sole ownership and control of a single person. Merrick had never taken in a partner and it was not until April 1925 that Coral Gables became a corporation.

Above: San Sebastian Apartments on University Drive and Lejeune Road, Paist and Steward Architects, Dec. 1926

At that time this corporation owned or controlled most of what is now the incorporated area of present-day Coral Gables, covering approximately 16 square miles or 10,000 acres (*Miami Herald,* April 29, 1925).

On April 29, 1925 the Florida Legislature created by charter the City of Coral Gables. Among other provisions, the charter specified that the city would be governed by a commission composed of Merrick, Baldwin, Knight, Webster, and Dammers, all of whom were officers of the Coral Gables Corporation. It further provided that the first election would be held on the second Tuesday in June 1929.

Coral Gables Today

Certainly the "Quality Of Life Within" envisioned by Merrick and his planners for his well planned city seems apparent when one travels through the many fine residential neighborhoods with lush mature landscaping and shaded, tree-lined streets. Certainly the efficient city plan and the strict zoning regulations have served

Above: Comprehensive bird's-eye map of Coral Gables showing proposed Cocoplum Beach, etc., Nov. 1925

to combat the many problems associated with the rapid expansion and growth which has occurred in Miami-Dade County during the last decade. In fact, Coral Gables was the first municipality in the county to enact an historic preservation ordinance on October 3, 1973 recognizing the historical values of a less than 50-year-old city at that time. This is a tribute to the pride that its approximately 45,000 citizens have for their special cultural heritage.

Today the downtown area of the city has grown to a new stature with the location of more than 150 multinational corporate offices attesting to Merrick's original vision for South Florida as the future "Port of the Americas." However, the presence of high rise buildings, garages, and their resulting architectural impact is causing continuous concern to the city in terms of what zoning policies should be enacted to accommodate this growth. In 1986 the "Mediterranean Architectural Ordinance" was passed which gave floor area bonuses to developers who would construct their mostly high-rise buildings with "Mediterranean" style motifs. This inducement of adding area and floors to their buildings has produced and is producing a

skyline featuring a variety of cupolas and other "Mediterranean" features. Both the current zoning and the "Mediterranean" ordinance are under review at the present time while many new building projects are ready to be implemented in the very vibrant downtown area of Coral Gables. A four-day public workshop called a "charrette" was held in 2002 which successfully engaged numerous citizen organizations and individuals in a dialogue over perceived problems and the future of the downtown area. It was sponsored by the City and the University of Miami and executed by the University of Miami School of Architecture.

— Aristides J. Millas

Statistical Areas within the City Limits of Coral Gables

Land

North of Sunset Road	4550	sq. ac.	7.11	sq. mi.
South of Sunset Road	3964	sq. ac.	6.19	sq. mi.
Total	8514	sq. ac.	13.3	sq. mi.

Water Canals and Waterways

North of Sunset Road	96	sq. ac.	.15	sq. mi.
South of Sunset Road	697	sq. ac.	1.09	sq. mi.
Bay Area	15296	sq. ac.	23.9	sq. mi.
Total	16089	sq. ac.	25.14	sq. mi.

Total Area	**24603**	**sq. ac.**	**38.44 sq. mi.**

Above: Entrance to proposed Exposition building in Crafts Section (unrealized), Sketch by Phineas Paist, 1924

Biscayne Bay

City Limits

Roadways

Waterways

Map 8
Coral Gables Today
Courtesy of Information
Technology Department

Note: Free city maps are available
at City Hall, 405 Biltmore Way

PART III

TOUR 1
CORAL GABLES
BUSINESS DISTRICT

∞

"Harmony in Business and Architecture"
—George E. Merrick

TOUR 1

Le Jeune
Road

Ponce de Leon

Douglas Road

● 15

Zamora

Madeira

Majorca

Navarre

● 10

Minorca

● 12

Alcazar

● 9   ● 13   ● 11

● 7

Alhambra
● 5   ● 6   ● 8   ● 11

Giralda

● 14   ● 17   ● 18

● 4   3 ● 21 22 ● 20

Aragon

● 2   ● 16   ● 19

● 1

Miracle Mile   ● 23

Andalusia   ● 25

Valencia   ● 24

Almeria

Sevilla   ● 26 ● 27

Palermo   ● 28

Catalonia

0   1/8 mile

Left: City Hall, Paist and Steward Architects, 1927

The 1921 map produced for the Coral Gables Corporation defines the commercial district's location along the axis of the Country Club Prado between Coral Way and Sevilla Avenue close to the western edge of the City's boundaries. It was described as a "notably attractive parked boulevard with rest seats to make it delightful while shopping."

As the development progressed however, the commercial and cottage industries were relocated to the eastern edge of the city in close proximity to already established communities, leaving the previously determined area exclusively for residential development. The Commercial Entrance to the City at Douglas Road and Alhambra Plaza was constructed in 1923 to serve as the point of entry into the business district.

The early buildings in the downtown area reflect the same studied approach to design as would be found in the residential areas. Commercial buildings also employed a variety of Mediterranean design characteristics. They often featured arcades at the street level that protected pedestrians from the weather and shaded them from the sun, and courtyards which provided welcome air and sunshine for both the customer and employee. In fact, decades later in 1986, the City Commission enacted the "Mediterranean Architectural Ordinance" that provided incentives in the central business district for those new developers who committed themselves to a "traditional" design approach.

Above: Coral Way looking west to City Hall, Feb. 1929

Coral Gables has suffered great losses of its original downtown buildings. The cause is economic; as land values rise exponentially, owners desire to make maximum use of their properties. As zoning increased density, the fate of many of the smaller, original buildings were doomed. The majority of the building stock in the downtown today dates from the 1950s and later when the commercial district came back into its own.

The "heart" of downtown is Miracle Mile, that part of Coral Way between LeJeune Road and Douglas Road. The credit for the renaissance of activity on Miracle Mile goes to George and Rebyl Zain. Mr. Zain, a public relations executive and Mrs. Zain, who became a Coral Gables City Commissioner, saw the potential in this broad avenue of retail shops. In 1944 they named the street "Miracle Mile," emulating other successful shopping districts around the country. They soon enticed the F.W. Woolworth company

and other stores to build major outlets in the city. The rest is history as today, fine retailers make their home along the Mile.

The tour route will take you a bit north and south of the central commercial district, but includes important community and educational buildings that are worth the trip.

Above: Administration Building, Coral Way and Ponce de Leon Boulevard, March 1925 (demolished)
Bottom: Sketch for new sales headquarters by Phineas Paist, Aug. 1925 (now part of Colonnade Hotel)

1 1950s

1
Coral Gables City Hall,
405 Biltmore Way,
1928, Harold Steward
and Phineas Paist,
Architects
Modeled after architect
William Strickland's 19th
century Philadelphia
Exchange Building.
The architects have
transplanted this
Neo-Classical icon to
the tropics. Note the
coral rock facing on
the base of the building,
and the indigenous flora
and fauna that make up
the whimsical capitals
of the columns.

2
John H. Stabile Building,
296 Aragon Avenue,
1924; Addition 1927,
John Davis, Architect
Originally this building
was used to manufac-
ture ornamental
concrete block that is
featured in so many
of the Mediterranean-
Revival residences in

3

Coral Gables. It remains
as one of the earliest
commercial structures in
the Downtown area,
and is presently used
as a bookstore.

3
Coral Gables Public
Safety Building,
285 Aragon Avenue,
1939, Phineas Paist,
Architect
Known to today's
residents as the "Old
Police and Fire Station,"
this is only one of two
buildings constructed
in Coral Gables by
the Public Works
Administration. The
PWA was one of the
agencies created by
President Roosevelt
to assist the nation in its
recovery from the Great
Depression. Although it
was built during an era
when Art Deco was the
reigning architectural
style, it is characteristi-
cally restrained and
again makes use of the
indigenous coral rock
geological substrate
of the area. Notice the
whimsical heads of
the firemen on the
Aragon side. The build-
ing housed the Coral
Gables fire and police
departments from
1939 until 1975 when
a new facility was
constructed.

4
Gables Grand Plaza,
353 Aragon Avenue,
1998, Bermello-Ajamil,
Architects
This apartment building
with retail shops on the
ground floor is the first
major apartment to
be constructed in the
Gables for decades.
Its great success reflects

the growing residential
population in the
Downtown, and the
mixed-use formula that
has been encouraged
by City officials.

5
Miami News Building,
(now Café Demetrio),
300 Alhambra Circle,
1925
This one-story corner
building illustrates the
scale and design
features of all the buildings that once were a
part of the Alhambra
Plaza streetscape.
Note the use of the

5 6 1925

tower to articulate the
corner, and the relief
ornament of the window
surrounds. Originally
the large fixed glass
panels were fenestrated
with a multi-paned type.

6
Coral Gables Garage
(now Washington
Mutual Bank),
290 Alhambra Circle,
1922, H. George Fink,
Architect
The building was origi-
nally constructed for a
car dealership selling
Hudson-Essex motor-
cars. The building
continued to be used as
a dealership, long after
the demise of those
cars, and later became
the popular Loeffler
Brothers Oyster House.

The garage bays are still visible on the façade, although enclosed to accommodate its new uses.

**7
Old Coral Gables City Hall (Now American Legion Post #98), 303 Alhambra Circle, c.1925**

The Florida land development boom had reached its zenith by 1926, and sales went downward from then on, drying up completely by 1928. Nonetheless, the optimistic leaders of Coral Gables completed their "new" City Hall at 405 Biltmore Way in 1927. Prior to the completion of the new City Hall, this building was used for the business of the City Commission.

**8
Alhambra International Center/ 201 Alhambra Circle, 255 Alhambra Circle, 1975 and 1976, O.K. Houston, Architect**

As modernism swept American cities in the 1970s, traditional designs were abandoned in favor of minimalist designs that featured great expanses of glass, and construction

technology that was celebrated in high rises. The Alhambra International Center and the adjacent 201 Alhambra Building, built one year later, were the wave of the future, and at the "cutting edge" of contemporary design. They were, however, an anomaly in Coral Gables, where there was a strong tradition of masonry buildings, where surface ornament and recognized traditional features added a great deal to overall design. Many refer to these buildings as a major catalyst for the creation of the city's Mediterranean Architectural Ordinance. The 1986 ordinance creates development bonuses for buildings that convey a traditional Mediterranean-inspired design.

**9
Hotel Place San Michel, 162 Alcazar Avenue, 1926, Anthony Zink, Architect**

Originally designed as a commercial building for retail sales, the building soon became a hotel. Today, the quaint individually decorated rooms offer an alternative to hotel chains. The restaurant is a favorite for breakfast meetings and elegant dinners.

**10
Coral Gables Elementary School, 105 Minorca Avenue, 1923–1926, Richard Kiehnel, Architect**

The first wing of this courtyard building was constructed in 1923 facing onto Minorca

10 1925

Avenue. Between the year of its construction and 1926, two additional wings were needed to accommodate the waves of new citizens arriving in droves. The gable roofed structure with an imposing two-story porch that fronts onto Ponce de Leon Boulevard houses the 900-seat auditorium.

**11
The Columbus Center, 1 Alhambra Plaza, 1990, Mitchell & Giurgola, Architects and the Hyatt Regency Coral Gables, 50 Alhambra Plaza, 1987, Nichols Brosch Sandoval, Architects**

These two buildings face each other across the wide boulevard of Alhambra Boulevard. Both are new additions to the city, and reflect two vastly different interpretations of the "Mediterranean Architectural Style." In the Columbus Center, the design is broad and stylized while the Hyatt is much more traditional in its use of a colonnaded loggia and cast ornament. Both reflect the desire on the part of the city to return to the traditions first established in the early development.

12 1926

12
**The Cla-Reina Hotel /
La Palma Hotel, 112-116
Alhambra Circle, 1924,
H. George Fink,
Architect; Rehabilitation
1994, Fullerton Diaz,
Architects**

Originally called the
Cla-Reina, the hotel
opened in 1924 and
is one of the classic
Mediterranean style
buildings that once
characterized the
entire city. The building
has since been
remodeled to serve
as an office building.

13 1925

13

13
**Alhambra Towers,
122 Alhambra
Circle, 2002,
The Allen Morris
Company, Developer,
John A. Cunningham,
Design Architect**

The Commercial
Entrance that leads to
this triangular parcel
has an amazing history.
It was first the location
of the Bank of Coral
Gables and Post
Office, a colonnaded
Mediterranean building
designed by Walter C.
De Garmo and
completed in 1924.
In 1954, the Danish
Modern First
Presbyterian Church
was built on the site,
actually incorporating
parts of the original
bank and post office.
The church was razed to
accommodate the new
office building which
completely fills the
triangular site with a
prominent tower projec-
tion at the apex of the
triangle. The tower
cupula is similar to that
of the Biltmore Hotel,
which was modeled
after the Giralda Tower
of the Cathedral of
Seville. The legacy of
the Church is main-
tained, as the Morris
Company salvaged
the stained glass panels
that illustrate the
passage in the 23rd
Psalm, and reinstalled
the panels in the lobby.
The effect is lyrical,
and while the functions
of a church and office
building seem to be
incongruous, the

Alhambra Towers
manages to combine
them artfully. It is a
fitting tribute to the
traditions in Coral
Gables' evolving history.

14
**The Dream Theater
(now Bank of America),
2308 Ponce de Leon
Boulevard, 1926,
John and Coulton
Skinner, Architects**

This building originally
served as an open-air
movie theater, but has
been successfully
adapted for the bank's
use. When it first
opened, newspaper
articles described the
building as an outdoor
movie theater designed
to resemble a Spanish
bullring, with a central
tower entrance and
shops. The Skinner
brothers were also the
architects for the
French Normandy
Village off LeJeune
Road and the Florida
Pioneer Village on
Santa Maria Street.

15
**The Coral Gables
Academy (now Merrick
Educational Center),
39 Zamora Avenue,
1926, John and Coulton
Skinner, Architects**

In keeping with the
desire to provide the
best in educational facilities, the Coral Gables
Academy was built to
add another dimension
to the already existing
schools. The architects
were also the architects
of the Dream Theater
downtown (see 14).

16
**First National Bank
of Coral Gables
(now El Ostoria del
Moro Restaurant),
2312 Ponce de Leon
Boulevard, 1926,
J.P. Turner, Architect**

This building survives
from the early days
of Coral Gables, and
illustrates the use of
classical architectural
themes in the small-scale
buildings of the day.

17
**H.N. Dietrich Hardware
(now United Airlines),
178 Giralda Avenue,
1926, Phineas Paist,
Architect**

Another of the surviving
early buildings, this was
designed by Phineas
Paist, who by 1925
had been named
"Supervising Architect"
for the entire city.
Mr. Paist signed off on
the design of every
building before it could
be constructed. Perhaps
his greatest achievement
was his collaboration
with Harold Steward
on the design for the
Coral Gables City Hall
at 405 Biltmore Way.

18
**Merrick Place, 290
Alhambra Circle, 1997,
Carr Smith Corradino,
Architects**

The City of Coral
Gables commissioned
the architects to design
a mixed-use building,
the bulk of which would
serve as a parking
garage. In a skillful
design, the building
takes on the pie shaped
lot with interesting
elevations on every
side that is decidedly
Mediterranean in spirit.
The shops and restau-
rants on the ground
floor have enjoyed
great success at
this location.

19
**The Colonnade
Building, now
Colonnade Hotel
and Office Building,
133–169 Miracle Mile,
1926, Original**

**Architects: Phineas
Paist, Walter De Garmo,
and Paul Chalfin,
Addition: 1987, Spillis
Candela & Partners**

The Colonnade Building
was constructed for
George Merrick's Coral
Gables Corporation
sales office. Occupying
a pivotal corner at
Miracle Mile and
Aragon Avenue, the
building embodied the
ideals of the entire
development, and
featured an arcade on
the ground floor and
a two-story entrance
portal that featured a
wealth of intricately
designed cast ornament.
The building was sub-
stantially completed
when the bottom fell
out of the real estate
market by early 1927.
Nonetheless the
building seemed to find
occupants throughout
its long history, but
by 1987 was showing
signs of deterioration.
The existing zoning laws
that allowed for buildings
substantially bigger
than the Colonnade
also threatened it.
In a winning solution
for all, the architects
designed a high rise
addition that would take
up the entire block and
contain the parking

garage to accommodate the new hotel and office uses. It remains one of Coral Gables' most important landmarks that has reinvented itself for a modern world.

20
Luminaire Building, 2331 Ponce de Leon Boulevard, 1993, Mateo and Rizzo, Architects

While there are incentives for new development to return to the classic Mediterranean style of early Coral Gables, there are some modern buildings that stand out as exemplary designs. The Luminaire Building is one that departs from any formula, making its own bold statement in a singularly original fashion. The building has been cited as a notable achievement in several national architectural magazines.

21 / 22
Books & Books and the Colson, Hicks, Eidson Building, 255–265 Aragon Avenue. Originally The Weiland Clinic, 1927, Lee Wade, Architect; Colson, Hicks, Eidson Building, 2000, Raul Rodriguez, Architect

These two buildings are paired in the discussion, as the Books & Books Building is a 1920s medical office building, and the building directly to the east is a new building that was designed to complement its historic neighbor. The original 20s building features a courtyard and is perfectly adapted as a very popular independent bookstore. It was originally the office of Dr. Arthur Weiland, an orthopedic surgeon. Weiland opened his clinic on January 1, 1928 with as many as six surgeons employed during the clinic's active practice.

The new mid-rise building to the east of the Clinic demonstrates another adaptation of the Mediterranean prototype, this time using an Italian Renaissance palazzo for its inspiration. The two buildings together represent the continuity that has spanned over seven decades.

23
The Miracle Theater, 280 Miracle Mile, 1947–48, William H. Lee (Philadelphia), Architect; Restoration, 1996, John Fullerton, Architect

The opening of the Miracle Theater was a huge event in Coral Gables, as it joined two other movie theaters in the City. Owned by the Wometco Theater chain, it was converted on two separate occasions, first for a two-plex, then as a four-plex. Still, with the advent of multi-plexes, the theater could not keep economic pace. The City of Coral Gables stepped up to the plate to prevent its demolition when the theater company sold it. For the first time in its history the city bought the building and charged The Actors Playhouse with its management. Actors Playhouse at the Miracle Theater has been an enormous success, bringing live theater to the heart of the city.

For its adaptation from a movie house into a performing arts center, architect Fullerton refitted the auditorium to accommodate an orchestra pit and sufficient stage and fly space to conduct theater. Much of the original, interior Art Deco ornament was restored.

24
The Coral Gables Bakery (now Le Maison L'Entrecote Restaurant), 2530 Ponce de Leon Boulevard, 1927, Phineas Paist, Architect

The Coral Gables Bakery was owned by members of the Peacock family, early Coconut Grove pioneers. George Merrick, the founder and developer of the City of Coral Gables, married Eunice Peacock in 1916. The Bakery building has not been significantly altered, and demonstrates the fine proportions and tasteful ornament that was the hallmark of the Mediterranean Revival buildings designed for the original city.

25
H. George Fink Studio Building, 2506 Ponce de Leon Boulevard, 1925, H. George Fink, Architect

Of all the remaining early buildings, the Fink Studio represents the paradigm of Mediterranean design. Architect H. George Fink, George Merrick's

cousin, was of preeminent importance in the early stages of development beginning in 1921. Fink lived and worked in this studio that features the picturesque Venetian Gothic arch in its design.

26
Union Planters Bank, 3001 Ponce de Leon Boulevard, 1999, Spillis Candela & Partners, Architects

This high rise takes maximum advantage of its frontispiece, the Ponce Circle/ Fred Hartnett Park. The plaza in the front "spills" out over the roadway, and achieves continuity with the Park.

27
Ponce Circle Park/ Fred Hartnett Park

Located in the heart of the Crafts Section, the Park was originally designed to hold a major exposition building that would showcase the wares of the businesses surrounding it. Today the park is a favorite for smaller events and exhibitions. It was renamed in honor of former mayor Fred Hartnett.

28
Coral Gables Arts Center Building (Originally Paist and Fink Studio now offices of Ferguson, Glasgow, Schuster and Soto, Architects), 2901 Ponce de Leon Boulevard, 1925, Phineas Paist, Architect

As did H. George Fink further north on Ponce de Leon Boulevard, architect Phineas Paist and artistic advisor Denman Fink chose to locate their studios in the commercial area. In fact, the Arts Center Building is located in the Crafts Section subdivision, intended as a mixed-use area where the local cottage industries could be showcased and where artisans lived above their stores. Note the characteristic use of the tower to articulate the corner in this Mediterranean style building.

PART III

TOUR 2
CORAL GABLES
THE EARLY HOMES

∽

"The Quality of Life Within"
—George E. Merrick

TOUR 2

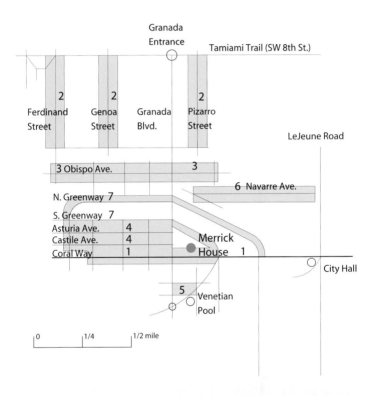

Granada Entrance

Tamiami Trail (SW 8th St.)

2
Ferdinand Street

2
Genoa Street

Granada Blvd.

2
Pizarro Street

LeJeune Road

3 Obispo Ave.

3

6 Navarre Ave.

N. Greenway 7

S. Greenway 7

Asturia Ave. 4

Castile Ave. 4

Coral Way 1

Merrick House

1

City Hall

5

Venetian Pool

0   1/4   1/2 mile

Opposite page: Sketch for home, by H. George Fink, 1922

A 1923 promotional piece called *Coral Gables Miami's Master Suburb* features a series of illustrated full pages that would capture the philosophy of early home development. They read "Leading Architects Design Coral Gables Homes," "Hundreds of Distinctive Homes," "Advantages of Spanish Architecture," and "Careful and Wise Building Restrictions." They explained that both the largest or smallest home would be carefully planned by a leading architect, that they would not be the type of houses you would find in the average building development, and that there were economic advantages which group building made possible. They boasted about the building of hundreds of homes in the previous year's development program and extolled the virtues to be found in the rare fidelity to the "Spanish" style. In every section visitors could witness the distinctive quality and beauty of the homes themselves. There were restrictions for the number of lots required for a particular size of house specified to designated streets. Minimum costs would range from $4,000 to $25,000. There were also set back and perimeter wall requirements written into the contract deed. Nothing would prevent the building of a modest home providing it was constructed of masonry block or tile with a stucco finish.

The early architects were very articulate in specifying the characteristics of this distinctive residential architecture they created in Miami's Master Suburb. In the 1923 *Miami Riviera* publication with photos of many of the houses constructed along with their owner's names, they would write:

> Consider first the conditions of South Florida itself, the terrain of Coral Gables which has made this architecture possible. The land is the floor of the world, wide and level, impressive as the sea that is its great neighbor and originator. Over it the vast dome of the sky pours a soft white radiance in which every leaf and bough and palmetto point is brilliantly visible for miles....The architects found that they could study the principles of the new Coral Gables architecture in that great district of southern Europe – the coast of the Mediterranean, which has been the fountainhead of architecture for centuries, a district unified in spite of the differences in history and race and locality, by the similarity of its climatic and living conditions.

The text illustrates the breadth of the architect's knowledge and depth of their deliberations as they refer to 19th century architects and theorists Viollet-le-duc, William Morris, and John Ruskin. After citing key Mediterranean architectural examples, they would continue...

The characteristics of the architecture of Coral Gables, then, are these: walls of tinted stucco, where also the native rock, warmed to cream and soft brown and old amber in the sun, is used as occasional window trim or ledge or wall finish, are raised to enclose rooms open at every side to the air. The rough surface of the walls catches the changing light, the shadows of decoration or leaf, until they seem a very part of the earth on which they are built...in a hundred inconspicuous ways these homes are made to seem to grow rather than be built.

Architect Phineas Paist, named "Supervisor of Color" for Coral Gables, borrowed from his experience at the James Deering estate ("Vizcaya") and wrote on the application technique of exterior stucco to obtain naturalistic and pleasing surfaces in *National Builder Magazine* (October 1924):

Stucco as applied in Coral Gables is unusually of a so-called "Spanish effect" which means that the scratch coat has been quickly and roughly troweled on about half an inch thick, followed almost immediately with a texture finish applied as a second coat troweled upon with accidental thicknesses and surfaces uneven in effect. Sometimes this second coat is knocked down or brushed to give an old weather worn texture...Usually the first coat of color is of some deep rich color, well waterproofed and completely covering and filling all of the stucco. This is followed by half tone colorings either gray or possible subsequent stucco coloring, then by a high light color wash.

Asturia Avenue in October 1926

The principles of color even went beyond individual buildings as Paist continued:

> In Coral Gables we have endeavored to use zone coloring; that is, certain portions of the development will have full rich coloring quite to the limit of our palette, while others will have gray zones; some streets have been worked from an almost pure white color, at one end flushed up into the rich coloring of interior zones at the other end. Streets have been studied house against house, so as to lead in what may be called "a tone symphony from cold to warm colors."

Merrick and his architects would also identify their concern for the roofs:

> which stand out against the sky, which bear only the sun....as a result, there is only a slight pitch to them. They must not gather heat. Highly glazed, cheap commercial tiles, slate or shingles are here highly impossible. Old hand-made Spanish tiles, soft glazed, blended in the loveliest browns and dull reds and ochres and siennas in the world, top the mellow walls with exactly the right emphasis. The sun is not harsh upon them, only infinitely at home. Their colors lead to the splendid harmonies of the awnings which shade the windows, awnings chosen by artists to blend not only with the whole picture of the house, but with the whole picture of the street, olive green and brown and mahogany and cream and orange and black – masterpieces, every one.

The architectural treatise concludes as follows:

> To study the homes of Coral Gables from their architectural point of view is to learn what has made great architecture everywhere, but even more than that it is to appreciate what fine thinking, what careful craftsmanship, what high artistic purpose, what exact adaptation to needs must go into the creation of an architectural style so unquestionably original and valuable as this of Coral Gables...And it is to realize with a new thrill that here a great new school of American architecture is created.

These excerpts reveal the depth of thought and creativity that Merrick and his architects gave to the homes of Miami's Master Suburb. By ensuring these high standards, the development would promise a quality of excellence that could not be achieved by competing real estate interests in this frenetic period of building in South Florida.

Opposite page top: Coral Gables Merrick House (1906), 907 Coral Way in 1925
Opposite page center: George Merrick's "Poinciana Place" (1916), 937 Coral Way in 1926
Opposite page bottom: House at 1924 Ferdinand Street in 1926

Tour Routes

This tour focuses on the streets where groups of the early, mostly speculative, original homes still exist. They have been identified from the compilation of early Sanborn Fire Insurance maps dating from June 1924 (page 27) which show the actual building footprints. One should look for the architectural characteristics previously described of details, texture, and composition in which no two small homes are exactly alike. Also notice the juxtaposition of the gabled roof, the shed roof, and the flat roof with a decorative chimney as an accent. This tour will also include "The Country Club of Coral Gables Historic District," named as a local historic district by the City Commission in September 1988. The district contains a significant number (59) of residences designed by architects who have made a substantial contribution to developing the character of the city. These residences encircle the Granada Golf Course with the Country Club (1923) as the focal point.

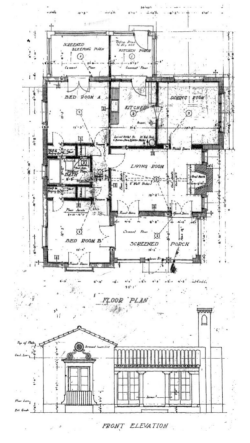

Cottage No. 8, 1028 Obispo Avenue, Walter De Garmo, Architect (plan and elevation)

1 Briggs residence 920 Coral Way, 1924

2 1102 Genoa Street, 1926

2 2703 Alhambra Circle, 1926

1 "Casa Azul" 1254 Coral Way, 1924

1
Coral Way
from Balboa Plaza, Anderson Road west to Madrid Street

The earliest homes of Coral Gables date back to the days of the plantation where the Merrick homestead is located at 907 Coral Way and listed in the National Register of Historic Places. The home, called "Coral Gables Merrick House," dates from 1906 and is constructed from local oolitic limestone (coral rock) and features a striking wrap-around veranda. The home actually incorporates the Merricks' wood frame cabin that was their home from 1899. Today the property is operated as a house-museum and is a must stop to experience an outstanding example of early Gables archi-tecture and family memorabilia. Coral Way is the main east-west artery of the city and the early homes were built for the Merrick family and friends. Close to the Merrick House at 937 Coral Way is Poinciana Place, the first home for George Merrick and his bride Eunice Peacock (1916) by architect H. H. Mundy. The original "Briggs" house (1916) at 920 Coral Way was designed by architect H. George Fink, Merrick's cousin. H. George Fink's own house (Casa Azul 1924) can be seen at 1254 Coral Way. The home of Doc Dammers, the first mayor (1924), is located at 1141 Coral Way. It was also designed by H. George Fink.

2
Ferdinand Street, Genoa Street, Pizarro Street to Milan Avenue

These are the north-south streets on which a significant number of homes were constructed, providing a physical visual impact for visitors to the Master Suburb from the "Tamiami Trail" (today's SW 8th Street). The Tamiami Trail was begun when Mr. Merrick was a county commis-sioner in 1916 (although it was not dedicated until 1928), and is the subject of one of his poems as well as the location of the first entrance gateway into the city to be constructed. The Granada Entrance is a fitting introduction to Granada Boulevard,

2 1510 Genoa Street, 1924

the main north-south axis of the suburb. Ferdinand Street is especially interesting in that it contains a number of two-story homes while Genoa and Pizarro Streets contain more of the single-story small cottages.

3
Obispo Avenue from Ferdinand Street eastward to Cortez Street
"Avenue Obispo" was the title of a promotional brochure in 1924 by George E. Merrick. It featured the photos of 33 homes that were constructed in less than five months and quickly

sold. A plan and elevation for one of these homes is illustrated on page 64. The drawing labeled "Cottage #8" and designed by Walter de Garmo is a superb example of the richness of detail applied to even the smallest of houses.

4
Asturia Avenue Castile Avenue from North Greenway Drive eastward to Granada Boulevard
These avenues contain many of the early homes.

5
The block across from the **Venetian Pool,** the

original quarry from which coral rock was used for the road beds and some building materials for the early homes bounded by **De Soto Boulevard, Valencia Street,** and **Granada Boulevard.**

6
Navarre Avenue from Pizarro Street eastward to LeJeune Rd.
It is on this street that the *News-Metropolis* sponsored a model of the "Ideal Home" in April 1924 which is illustrated here. It is still standing at 716 Navarre.

3 1236 Obispo Avenue, 1926

3 1131 Obispo Avenue, 1926

6 "Ideal Home" 716 Navarre Avenue 1924

7 Third Merrick Residence 832 S. Greenway Drive 1925

7
"The Country Club of Coral Gables Historic District"

North Greenway Drive from Segovia Street westward to Granada Boulevard where the Country Club is situated, then westward, circling down to South Greenway Drive, then eastward, crossing Granada Boulevard to Balboa Plaza at Coral Way and Anderson Road.

7 Residence on 1126 S. Greenway Drive 1926

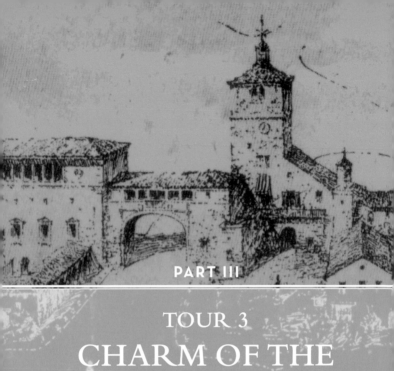

TOUR 3
CHARM OF THE
ROADWAY

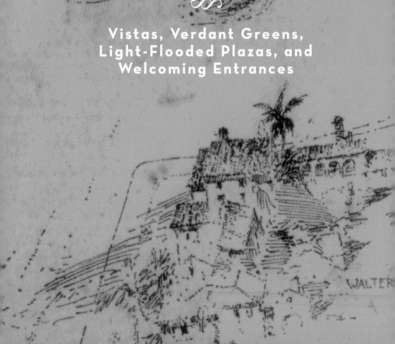

Vistas, Verdant Greens,
Light-Flooded Plazas, and
Welcoming Entrances

TOUR 3

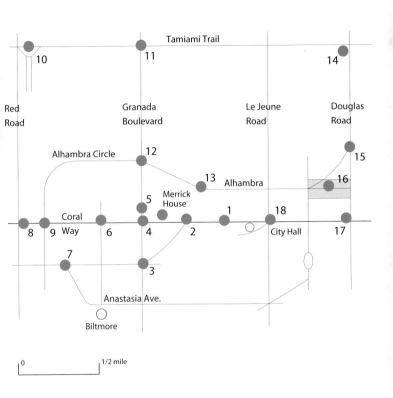

Tamiami Trail

10 11 14

Red Road Granada Boulevard Le Jeune Road Douglas Road

Alhambra Circle 12 15

13 Alhambra 16

5 Merrick House 1 18

Coral Way 6 4 2 City Hall 17

8 9 7 3

Anastasia Ave.

Biltmore

0 1/2 mile

Opposite page: Douglas Entrance drawing, De Garmo, Fink, and Paist

Coral Gables remains today as it was envisioned, a great open-air garden under a dazzling sky. The city, with its generous, luxuriant green spaces becomes a park in which are placed buildings, and not the other way around. In a 1927 promotional piece entitled *A Great American City Region* the legendary environmentalist Marjorie Stoneman Douglas used this exquisite prose to describe this special place:

> To drive about Coral Gables is constantly to be discovering new charms of roadways, new vistas of great distance, new tunnels of green which open out to light flooded plazas, new curving perspectives of trees and charming roofs and great lifts of sky.

In a further enhancement of this already picturesque scheme, Denman Fink, the artistic advisor of Coral Gables, envisioned grand entrances that would mark the major entrances into the city. In a very concrete way, these entrances immediately define the permeating concepts for the city. They are substantial, built of the indigenous coral rock and Dade County pine, are weathered and appear to have existed for eons, and are presumably inspired by similar gateways found in Spain and Italy.

In all there were fourteen plazas and seven major entrances. While most of the plazas were incorporated into the completed plan, only four of the entrances were completed. Your drive will take you past fountains and pergolas, piers and loggias, all designed for their sheer beauty and as a compliment to this lush landscape. Though the first roads in Coral Gables were not constructed until 1921, just four years later there were over 100 miles of roadway linking the developing city.

Alhambra Circle became the longest roadway. It begins at Douglas Road (SW 37th Avenue) and winds its way through some dramatic landscapes and period homes. Coral Way is the major east-west artery in the city with some of the city's oldest homes alongside. Coral Way is particularly worth the drive with its mature live oaks and banyans creating a sun-dappled canopy and the variety of plazas that occur at almost every major intersection.

1
**Segovia Plaza,
Coral Way, North
Greenway Drive, and
Segovia Street**
The piers, walls, and wall
fountains that frame
North Greenway Drive
lead to the Granada
Golf Course, a nine hole
public course. The area
is particularly important
in the growth of the
city, as the nearby
Coral Gables Country
Club was the "nerve
center" where city father
George Merrick first
entertained his prospec-
tive clients. The drive
along North and South
Greenway Drives is
one of the most beautiful
in the city, and has
been named a local
historic district.

2
**Balboa Plaza,
Coral Way, Anderson
Road, DeSoto
Boulevard, and South
Greenway Drive**

3
**De Soto Plaza,
Sevilla Avenue,
Granada, and
De Soto Boulevards**

4 1926

This intersection that
features a monumental
freestanding fountain in
the center is a favorite
of visitors and natives
alike. The fountain, a
pedestal type that
supports an obelisk,
features relief carvings
of four faces which each
contain a fountain jet.

4
**Ponce de Leon Plaza,
Coral Way, and
Granada Boulevard**
This plaza was the first
of the planned fourteen
plazas to be constructed.
Designed by Denman
Fink and built in 1921,
the plaza measures
600 feet in diameter.
At four points adjacent
to the open space,
Fink has designed
fountain pools, fountains,
and pergolas.

5
**Castile Plaza,
Granada Boulevard,
and Castile Avenue**

6
**Columbus Plaza,
Columbus Boulevard,
and Indian Mound Trail**

6 1924

Although smaller in
scale than others, this
plaza's features are the
same as those used
throughout the city.
The first water tower
can be seen in the
distance (in the photo).

3 1926

7
Plaza San Domingo, Anastasia Avenue, and Sevilla Avenue

8
Coral Gables Garden Club Entrance, Red Road (SW 57th Avenue and Coral Way)

The city's original plans called for the "Gladeside Entrance" to be built at this location. It was never constructed, nor have drawings survived to tell us what it would have looked like. The two wall fountains, piers, and walls that flank Coral Way as it meets SW 57th Avenue (the western terminus of the city's boundaries), was a gift of the Coral Gables Garden Club. The Club has embarked on an ambitious plan to build decorative features in the tradition of the original entrances and plazas at those originally planned locations.

9
Augustine Plaza, Coral Way, Alhambra Circle, and Country Club Prado

10
Country Club Prado Entrance, Tamiami Trail (SW 8th Street), and Country Club Prado

Of all the entrances to the city, this is the most magnificent, and represents the most varied treatment. The roadways entering here allow the opportunity for the creation of a grassy triangular space that is framed by monumental piers leading to the centerpiece.

10 1926

11 1924

Here two pedestal fountains terminate the north and south ends of the expansive rectangular mirror pool that is flanked by vine and flower covered pergolas.

11
Granada Entrance, Granada Boulevard, and Tamiami Trail (SW 8th Street)

Constructed in 1922, this was the first of the seven entrances planned for the city. Reported to be inspired by similar entrance gates in Spain, the 340-foot-long structure features a 40-foot arch that spans Granada Boulevard.

12
Granada Plaza, Alhambra Circle, and Granada Boulevard

In another Denman Fink plaza wall, fountains are added to sitting ledges that invite pedestrians to enjoy the water element.

13
Alcazar Plaza, Alhambra Circle, and Casilla Street

14
Douglas Entrance Tamiami Trail (SW 8th Street) and Douglas Road (SW 37th Avenue) Restoration and additions in the 1980s: Spillis Candela & Partners, Architects

The last entrance to be completed in 1927, the Douglas Entrance was built at a cost of a million dollars. By 1927 the real estate boom had collapsed, and the original vision for the Douglas Entrance was not realized. The complex was to have covered over 10 acres with a series of buildings that featured towers and arcades built to suggest the quintessential image of a town square.

14 1926

14 1927

17
Coral Gables Garden Club Entrance Douglas Road (SW 37th Avenue) and Miracle Mile (Coral Way)

The original name for this entrance was the "Bayside Entrance" which was never constructed.

Douglas Road is the eastern terminus of the city's boundaries. The monument with a fountain feature on either side of Miracle Mile was a gift of the Coral Gables Garden Club, as one of a series of monuments to be built at the originally planned locations.

18
LeJeune Plaza, LeJeune Road, and Coral Way

Lejeune Road is named for a pioneer plantation owner. The plaza terminates the axis of Coral Way at the City Hall site where Biltmore Way begins its route to the landmark hotel. Only the eastern walls and fountains of the plaza remain, and a lamp post on the west.

What was built is still impressive, and today recently constructed office buildings surround the original entrance, creating a commercially viable use for the land.

15
Commercial Entrance Douglas Road and Alhambra Circle

The stone mason for this entrance leading to the commercial core was Charles Merrick, brother of the city's founder. It was the second entrance to be constructed in 1923 and features a 600-foot-long wall and stone archway that is reminiscent of ancient Roman prototypes.

16
Alhambra Plaza, The block between Douglas Road and Alhambra Circle

15 1926

PART III

TOUR 4

THE VILLAGES

The Architecture Of The World
Arrives in Coral Gables

TOUR 4

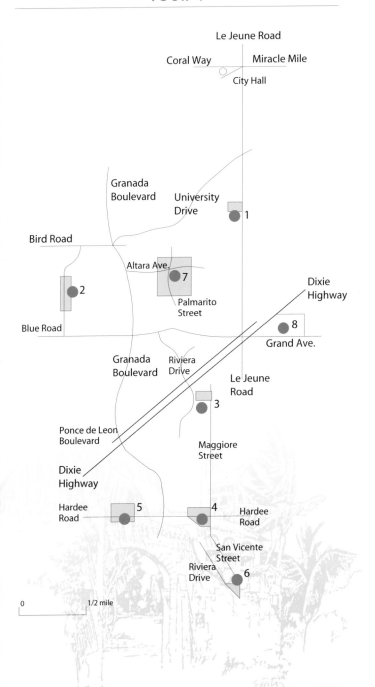

Le Jeune Road

Coral Way   Miracle Mile

City Hall

Granada
Boulevard   University
Drive   1

Bird Road
                      Altara Ave.
                                          7

                                   Palmarito
                  2   Street   Dixie
                                                                Highway

Blue Road
                                                    8
                                          Grand Ave.

Granada   Riviera
Boulevard   Drive   Le Jeune
                                    Road

Ponce de Leon   3
Boulevard

                                   Maggiore
Dixie   Street
Highway

Hardee   5   4   Hardee
Road   Road

                           San Vicente
                           Street
                  Riviera   6
                  Drive

0   1/2 mile

Opposite page: Aerial rendering, French City Village, Mott Schmidt, Architect, 1925

When the Riviera Section and the University of Miami were announced in 1925, which would almost double the size of Coral Gables, there were many ambitious planning components in its composition, the foremost being the University of Miami. Other components would be a Mahi Shrine Temple, golf course and sports center (not constructed), University High School (constructed), Florida East Coast Railway Station and concourse (not constructed), Sanitarium and Hospital (not constructed), fifty miles of paved streets and boulevards, and six miles of waterway frontage *"developed in Venetian beauty."* The housing concept for these areas would follow shortly and be promoted in the 1925 *Coral Gables Miami Riviera* booklet under the heading "Leading Architects Design Coral Gables Homes." The approach represented here would articulate a distinctly different concept in housing for the Master Suburb than originally envisioned. Nationally known architects were utilized under the direction of Denman Fink, Supervisor of Color; Phineas Paist, Supervisor of Architecture (appointed in May 1925); and Paul Chalfin, Consulting Architect (who was principally responsible for James Deering's Vizcaya estate).

Certainly the original Coral Gables architects headed by H. George Fink were not thinking about "themed" architecture when they wrote earlier in the 1923 *Coral Gables Miami Riviera*...

> The homes of Coral Gables then are noteworthy as a new development of American architecture. They represent the solution of a unique problem. It would have been easier for their architects to have copied lavishly good things which have been built in more ancient places...(with examples)...for the directing intelligence behind the whole creation of Coral Gables wisely and rightly understood that in its future lay the opportunity of developing a great new architecture, American because it was living and original, unique because it could express the most unique region in America, sub-tropical Florida.

Housing in the Riviera Section would diverge from this approach to a new American architecture and rely on identifiable models from around the country and the world. The themes and their locations were identified in the Contract Deeds and included The Florida Pioneer Type, Venetian Country Type, French Country House Type, Mexican Pioneer or Hacienda Type, Dutch African Pioneer Type, Dutch East Indian Pioneer Compound Type, Spanish Pioneer or Mission Type, Venetian Town or Canal Houses, Persian Canal Houses, Persian Village Type, Neopolitan Baroque Type, African Bazaar Type, Tangier Village Type, and the Chinese Compound Type.

The remaining blocks not stipulated for themed architecture went back to the trusted stylistic formula, described by the team as Spanish, Venetian, Moorish, Italian, or other similarly harmonious types of architecture.

The concept of themed architecture is not new to suburban planning that sought to promote harmonious design by frequently employing pre-existing regional types. Themed architecture was utilized in the Shaker Village planned community (incorporated 1911 and later called Shaker Heights) by the Van Sweringens. Their development near the city of Cleveland was specifically mentioned as having great influence on George Merrick in an interview he gave to the *Jacksonville Times Union* in January 1925. The Van Sweringens would build model homes in the 1920s in several English, Colonial, and French styles with detailed color schemes for each. Similar French and Colonial styles would be used in the Coral Gables Villages.

The sheer number and variety of the themed villages in George Merrick's development of Coral Gables is remarkable. In 1925, Merrick deeded hundreds of acres of land worth over $75 million to the American Building Corporation and the Myers Y. Cooper Construction Company. Cooper was a former Ohio state governor. In a promotional booklet, the project was described in this way. "Seven Miami architects and five New York architects are uniting in working out the details of the great planning of house construction. Thirteen styles are being used, drawn from various regions and nations which harmonize with the Mediterranean style now in use."

Aerial rendering, French City Village, Mott Schmidt, Architect, 1925

The Villages were to have contained over 1,000 homes, but only 80 were actually constructed. Confidence in the Florida Land Boom was exhausted by late 1926, and as a result, only seven of the fourteen villages were actually constructed. Even those that were constructed were on a greatly reduced scale. One can only wonder at the romantic imagery the city would have conveyed if all of the planned villages were actually constructed.

On February 1, 1927 *The Miami Herald* printed the observations of a Pulitzer-prize-winning journalist John J. Leary. Leary reported that the American Building Corporation of Cincinnati, Ohio had already completed a number of homes in seven different types of architecture and the number of homes completed in each type: "It begins with....The Florida Pioneer, a style based upon the aristocratic Georgia Colonial is perhaps the most truly American architecture in Coral Gables. Five homes of this type have been completed on Santa Maria Drive by the Myers Y. Cooper Company who do the construction for the American Building Corporation." The article continues to point out five homes of the 18th century French style, two Italian country houses by Robert L. Weed and five more nearby, a Venetian Waterway house by Phineas Paist, "built in one of the canals in such a way that they are reflected in the water," five homes of the Dutch South African type, and six homes of the Chinese Compound type. Also mentioned is the small French village on LeJeune Road.

Although this community was not part of the themed villages in the formal plan, the MacFarlane Homestead Subdivision is rightfully included here as an enclave with its own distinctive character and geographic boundaries. The decade of 1920s continued an age of racial intolerance. Around the country, it remained within the law to exclude African-Americans from living in certain communities. This led to the creation of separate communities that were actually self-sufficient, providing for not only houses, but churches and commercial establishments as well.

In Coral Gables, an area of approximately 20 acres directly south of U.S. Highway 1 was established exclusively for African-Americans. Many of those residents had emigrated from the Bahamas in the 1890s, taking up residency in Coconut Grove directly adjacent to the MacFarlane Homestead Subdivision. The housing types reflect their traditions and it is the only area in Coral Gables where wood-frame construction was allowed. Most of the homes were built in the 1920s and 1930s, and were occupied by a work force of skilled craftsmen and laborers that provided the means to build the "Master Suburb."

1
The French Normandy Village, LeJeune Road and Viscaya Avenue, 1926-27, John and Coulton Skinner, Architects

The original plan for this enclave called for 71 units to be built, however, only 11 were actually constructed. Brothers John and Coulton Skinner "borrowed" the half-timbering, shingled gables roofs, dormers, and projecting second story sections from architectural characteristics of the French provinces in the 15th and 16th centuries. During the 1930s this village was home to students at the University of Miami, as the buildings were used for the men's dormitories.

2
The Florida Pioneer Village, John and Coulton Skinner, Architects, Santa Maria Street, 1925

Using a Southern Colonial architectural vocabulary, John and Coulton Skinner designed this assemblage of homes that are set behind the Riviera Golf Course. The homes actually constructed in this group were never identical, but featured common characteristics which included their two-story form, pedimented porches with wooden rail details, shutters, bulls-eye windows, and other colonial-inspired decorative motifs. The architects chose to name this group the "Florida Pioneer Village," perhaps to distinguish it from any other Southern Colonial models.

3
The Chinese Village, 5100 block Riviera Drive/ Maggiore Street, 1926, Henry Killam Murphy, Architect

Henry Killam Murphy was a scholar of Oriental architecture. He was a published author on the subject, as well as a visiting professor in the Yale-in-China program.

These elaborately detailed houses with their brilliant primary hues more accurately reflect the character of temple design rather than of domestic houses. These flamboyant, signature pieces use such

3 1927

traditional Chinese devices as moon gates, upturned rafters and prominent roof ridges, glazed roof tiles, and simulated bamboo inserts in the "compound" wall, to convey the uniqueness of their design, unequalled elsewhere in the city, and perhaps the nation.

2 1926

4
French Country Village, 500 Block Hardee Road, 1926, Edgar Albright, Philip Goodwin and Frank Forster, Architects

The original plans called for the entire length of Hardee Road to be designed with houses of an "18th Century French Village" type. Again, this grand scheme failed to be realized in its entirety, but two components of that plan were constructed in part. Because of the more rustic nature of the houses in the 500 block historians have described them as "Country" to distinguish them from the formal French designs found in the 1000 Block, dubbed "City." The homes in the French Country Village exhibit a greater variation in individual designs than some of the more homogenous groups (e.g., The Chinese Village, The Dutch South African Village) Notice in particular the corner residence with its prominent tower entry and slate roof, as compared to another corner home that uses red brick and stone door and window surrounds and a flat variegated red tile roof to create a more "countrified" look.

5
French City Village, 1000 Block, Hardee Road, 1926, Mott Schmidt, Phillip Goodwin, Architects

An elaborate perimeter wall that rises to over nine feet in some places, and is articulated at the corners with pavilion-like structures unites these detached

5 1927

5 1927

6 | 1926

single-family homes. Although similar in their rectangular two-story form, great attention has been paid to the detailing of each home, so that they each possess a singular character. Across the road are larger individual residencies in the French style.

6
Dutch South African Village, Lejeune Road/Maya Avenue, Marion Syms Wyeth, 1926, Architects

The inspiration for this design comes from the homes built by Dutch settlers in South Africa during the 17th century. The elaborate parapets and spiral chimneys capture elements from their Boer counterparts. Wyeth was a renowned architect in his day, and had worked with Addison Mizner in the development of Palm Beach and Boca Raton.

7
The Italian Village, generally bounded by San Antonio & San Esteban Avenues, Montserrate and Palmarito Streets, 1926, A. L. Klingbeil, John and Coulton Skinner, R. L Ware, and Robert Law Weed, Architects.

Because of the larger geographic area covered, and the amount of infill between the Village houses, the Italian Village is less easily perceived as a "village." The corner of Altara and Montserrate contains several homes which best illustrate the driving principles in this group. The houses are built at a zero foot lot line, and follow the curve of the street. In plan they feature a courtyard that is flanked by the living quarters. There is a complexity of massing expressed in the variety of roofs slopes, and the use of one- and two-story elevations.

8
MacFarlane Homestead Subdivision Historic District, bounded by Oak Avenue on the north, Grand Avenue on the south, Brooker Street on the east and highway U.S. 1 on the west.

This historic district, listed in both the local and National Registers, is named for the subdivision platted by early pioneer woman Flora MacFarlane. It is unique to Coral Gables as it was the only area in the city where African-Americans were allowed to live. The district is directly adjacent to another African-American enclave that is within the boundaries of the City of Miami, and locally known as Coconut Grove. This area was the heart of the Bahamian settlement that grew up during the 1890s and later.

The district is primarily residential, although St. Mary's Baptist Church constructed in 1927 commands a presence in the neighborhood. Many of the homes are constructed of wood and reflect traditional African-American and Bahamian building types and are modest in scale. The "shot gun" style home is comprised of a narrow one-story, one-room wide house with a hall that runs its length. The other common house type is the bungalow, popular in the United States beginning in the last decade of the 19th century, that is also one-story in height, features a full width porch and is undecorated except for the exposed building parts such as the exposed rafters.

8 | typical "shot gun" home

PART III

TOUR 5

THE UNIVERSITY
OF MIAMI CAMPUS

∞

"The Great Out Door University"
—George E. Merrick

TOUR 5

San Amaro Drive

Granada Blvd.

Ponce de Leon Boulevard ↑

0   800 feet

Opposite page: sketch, Memorial Classroom Building, Manley and Weed Architects, 1947
This page bottom: sketch, Housing Complex, Manley and Weed Architects, 1947

The University of Miami originated with the beginning of Coral Gables in 1921 with promotional literature from George E. Merrick as he began the development of Miami's Master Suburb, and from others such as William Jennings Bryan who felt that this would be the perfect location for a great Pan-American university. The university was actually founded in 1925 and was the centerpiece of the Riviera Section (and the University of Miami) announcement, with many splendid visionary sketches of the intended building units, in the "Spanish" style, with their reflections in the proposed waterways and lake. *Newest Facts About Coral Gables* in April 1926

would announce, "The greatest educational project in the South, the University of Miami will see its first Administration and Arts and Science building completed in time to inaugurate the old Greek system of outdoor education with the October term of 1926. Also the Music and Art units will be built in 1926." It was promoted as the "Great Outdoor University at Coral Gables" which was featured on its stationery letterhead and other advertisements. In May 1926 construction was begun on the first building called the Solomon G. Merrick Building in honor of George Merrick's father. The university officially opened in October 1926 with 980 students. The first classes were held in the Anastasia Building, originally designed as a hotel and located off the present campus. This was only one month after the Hurricane of 1926 which devastated the Miami area leaving the first building a concrete skeleton when construction was halted. It would remain that way until the conclusion of World War II when the university was flooded with new students, especially ex-military personnel. Based on the sudden increase in enrollment President Bowman Foster Ashe hired Robert Law Weed and Marion I. Manley to develop a campus plan and building designs for the university. The original campus plan in the Spanish Renaissance style of Denman Fink and Phineas Paist was abandoned for a more contemporary and innovative plan with International Style buildings that were representative of the time period and the progressive direction of the university.

Elevation, reconstruction of proposed Merrick Building © R. Llanes

Actually this complete and bold campus plan was a great victory for modern architecture. The buildings for the campus were published in the prestigious *Architectural Forum* in 1948, 1949, and again in 1953. International recognition would be achieved with complete coverage in the widely circulated journal *L'Architecture D'aujourd'hui*, in December 1948. Both journals would feature drawings of the original intentions of Fink and Paist, to compare with the bold new designs by Weed and Manley and with detailed sections showing climatic concerns for the new buildings. Actually a completely modern campus for the Illinois Institute of Technology in Chicago was designed by Mies van der Rohe, architect and director of the institute in 1940, but the first buildings were not completed until after the Miami campus plans were announced.

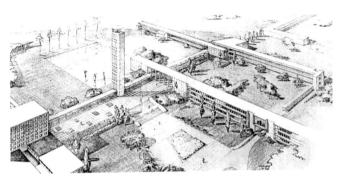

Tour Route

The main entrance to the university is on stately, palm-lined Stanford Drive and Ponce de Leon Boulevard. Metered visitor parking (P) can be found in front of the Lowe Art Museum, which was established in 1952 as the Joe and Emily Lowe Art Gallery. From here a walking route will highlight some of the earliest buildings, which are associated with the university's growth and expansion and have retained their integrity and architectural significance. The university opened its doors in 1926 and recently observed its 75th anniversary, however, the buildings on campus date from 1947. The young University of Miami is an exciting repository of 1950's and 1960's architecture which currently has a national focus in historic preservation research and dialogue. The current campus has successfully fulfilled one aspect of George Merrick's original vision and that would be as a botanical garden of stately royal palms and winding shaded pathways.

Aerial sketch, Campus Master Plan central group showing library, administration and classroom building, Manley and Weed Architects, 1947

1 Merrick Building in 1951

2 Memorial Classroom Building in 1951

1
Merrick Building
Walking from the traffic circle turn right and follow the university waterway passing under the School of Business Administration (1980) with additions (1995 and 2003), turn left at the fountain plaza and face the Merrick Building (1950) by architect Robert M. Little in the much heralded International style of the time with the most notable feature being the six story tower. This building's history dates back to the inception of the University of Miami when George Merrick began construction in May 1926 in honor of his father Soloman Merrick. The original plans were by Phineas Paist and the unfinished concrete and steel skeleton stood for over 20 years.

2
Memorial Classroom Building
Continue through the main green space of the campus defined by the 680 foot long Memorial Classroom Building (1947) by architects Marion I. Manley, the first registered woman architect in Florida, and Robert Law Weed, who were also responsible for the widely publicized Master Plan for the newly conceived university campus. This was the first building to be implemented in the plan and stood adjacent to the many wooden "shacks" where classes were previously taught. In November 1950 *The National Geographic Magazine* would do a main feature about the country's most modern university campus with an enrollment of 11,000, reporting that "No interior halls wind through this new Memorial

3 Art Building First Administration Building, © C. Penebad

Classroom Building. Breezes sweep into the lecture rooms across the open decks, keeping average indoor temperatures in this tropical climate at 75.2 degrees F." The building received a *Progressive Architecture* Award of Merit in 1948. Across from the Memorial Classroom Building stands the Ashe Administration Building by Watson & Deutchman (1954) and at the end of the green is the McArthur Engineering Building by Wahl Snyder & Associates with its brise-soleil (sun screen) (1959).

3
Art and Communication Building

Continue past the Engineering Building and you come to a group of wooden frame vernacular structures around a shaded natural "sinkhole." These represent the first temporary structures for the new campus cleverly pieced together from surplus army barracks buildings by Marion Manley and Robert Law Weed. They are the L-1 Communication Building (the first cafeteria building), the Art Building (the first administration building where Dr. Bowman Ashe had his office), and the Arts Annex Building, all dating from 1947. The most impressive is the long Art Building with its gallery walkway on the south side. It appears to be the prototype for the environmentally sensitive Memorial Classroom Building which Manley and Weed also designed. Unfortunately the university has this historic building scheduled for demolition but has supported its documentation for inclusion into the Historic American Building Survey (HABS).

We are including a photo with this publication.

4
Aboretums

Continue past the Art Building and into the John Clayton Gifford Arboretum established in 1950 by the Gifford Society of Tropical Botany. This is the first botanical garden established on the northernmost edge of the campus near the original administration building and contains over 500 species of plants. Other more recent arboretums on campus are the Palmetum (1999) located on the southeast side of the Memorial Classroom Building and the Florida Keys Satellite Arboretum (1997) located on the western edge of Lake Osceola. Turning left into the service drive of the Cox Science Building with long exposed concrete overhangs by Caudell Rowland and Scott

(1967) is yet another botanical project. It is the Taylor Alexander Microbiome Natural Pond Project (1999) created by the Florida Nurserymen and Growers Association.

5
Otto G. Richter Library
Continue on the walkway between the Cox Science Building and the Engineering Building across Memorial Drive to the covered passageway-breezeway of the Otto G. Richter Library by Watson, Deutshman and Kruse (1962), with its imposing book stack tower.

6
Jerry Herman Ring Theater
Continue over to the Miller Drive circle, pass the Gusman Concert Hall (1972) by architect Morris Lapidus to the unique Jerry Herman Ring Theater (1951) by architects Robert M. Little and Marian I. Manley. This building was designed with economic and flexibility considerations in mind. The building was capable of five theater seating arrangements and had innovative exterior and interior

7 Alfred Pick Music Library

design treatments including a concrete dome roof. It was featured in the 1953 *Progressive Architecture* and many other architectural journals. The original front entrance design has been altered.

7
Volpe Classroom Building and Alfred Pick Music Library
Continue walking along the side of the Ring Theater to Lake Osceola which forms the central space and image of this tropical campus. A central lake was always part of the university's conceptual image. It was originally to have been in front of the Merrick Building but placed in its current location to separate the housing areas from the academic and administrative acres in the Manley/Weed Master Plan. Next to

the Ring Theater is the School of Music. The early buildings of note are the Volpe Classroom Building (1954) with cantilevered stairways, and the cylindrical Alfred Pick Music Library (1958) with exposed steel structure. Both were designed by Robert M. Little.

8
Dormitory Buildings and School of Architecture
Continue counter clockwise around the lake to Architecture Buildings 48 and 49 located between the McDonald residential tower (1969) and Eaton Residence Hall (1954). These two buildings are the only ones facing the lake from the vast original housing complex of 27 buildings on 60 acres designed for the university by Manley and Weed in 1947 to house approximately 2000 students. They were funded by an almost five million dollar loan provided by the Federal Housing Administration to house primarily returning veterans and their families after World War II. These interlocking long and low buildings of sev-

6 Jerry Herman Ring Theater in 1951

8 Aerial view of dormitory complex 1951

8 Dormitories in 1951

8 School of Architecture

eral types display very strong characteristics of the International Style and were also designed to accommodate the demands of the tropical climate with characteristic concrete eyebrows above the windows. They pre-date Walter Gropius' Graduate Student Center at Harvard by more than two years. Less than half of the original buildings remain and they can be seen along Dickinson Drive east to Merrick Street which one can follow returning to the parking area in front of the Lowe Art Museum. Buildings 48 and 49 were retrofitted for the School of Architecture by architect Jan Hochstim when it moved to this location in 1984.

"THE PLACE WHERE A UNIVERSITY IS ESTABLISHED SHOULD BE ONE OF GOOD AIR AND BEAUTIFUL SURROUNDINGS, SO THAT SCHOLARS WHO IMPART WISDOM AND THE STUDENTS WHO RECEIVE IT FROM THEM MAY REST AND RECEIVE DELIGHT WHEN THEY RISE, AND THEN IN THE EVENING, WHEN THEY TIRE FROM THEIR STUDIES."

Alfonso X. El Sabio, King of Spain
(reigned 1252–1284)

From a bronze plaque mounted on Memorial Classroom Building (1947)

PART III

TOUR 6
THE COMMUNITY AMENITIES

A City of Inspiration, Culture, and Recreation

TOUR 6

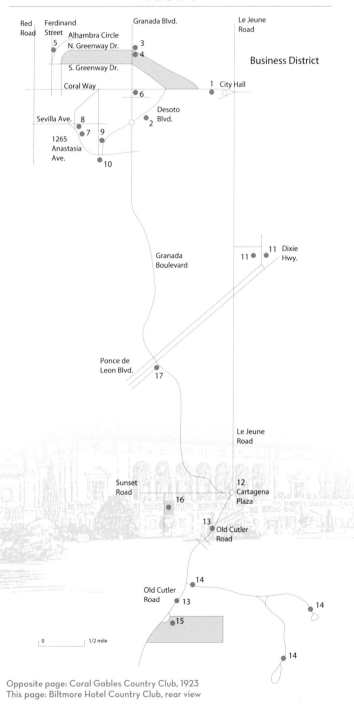

Red Road
Ferdinand Street
Alhambra Circle
N. Greenway Dr.
S. Greenway Dr.
Coral Way
Sevilla Ave.
1265 Anastasia Ave.
Granada Blvd.
Desoto Blvd.
Le Jeune Road
Business District
City Hall
Granada Boulevard
Dixie Hwy.
Ponce de Leon Blvd.
Le Jeune Road
Sunset Road
Cartagena Plaza
Old Cutler Road
Old Cutler Road

0   1/2 mile

Opposite page: Coral Gables Country Club, 1923
This page: Biltmore Hotel Country Club, rear view

The definition of community was especially important to George Merrick as he planned his ideal suburb. His own personal experiences and values led him to insure that Coral Gables would have the finest of educational and cultural facilities, and give his residents access to the abundant opportunities for leisure in this sun-filled paradise of South Florida.

Merrick after all, was the son of a Congregational minister, and had deep convictions born of his faith. He would donate the land for the first church to be completed in the city, the Coral Gables Congregational Church. Understanding the diversity of faiths, Merrick would also donate the land for the construction of the Catholic congregation's Church of the Little Flower. By 1925 Baptist, Presbyterian, and Universalist faiths had established themselves in Coral Gables.

As a young poet, Merrick was captivated by the written word and would make educational opportunities a priority for his community. In October 1924 the first phase of the Coral Gables Elementary School was opened and in 1925 the Ponce de Leon High School followed suit. Coral Gables Military Academy offered another kind of educational experience as did the Academy of Saint Joseph administered by the Sisters of St. Joseph. By October 1926 there were over 3,100 students enrolled in all levels of education in Coral Gables.

In addition to the schools and churches that advanced the goal of establishing community, the recreational opportunities enhanced it even further. The Granada Golf Course and Coral Gables Country Club were open by 1923, and were the epicenter for the entertainment of potential residents to the city. The centerpiece for the new city would be a magnificent hotel and country club in the heart of the Riviera Section. That centerpiece, still in operation today, is the Biltmore Hotel and Country Club.

Tahiti Beach, a microcosm of a South Sea village on the shore of Biscayne Bay, was directly linked to the construction of the Biltmore Hotel. But in terms of finding an ideal bathing experience nothing could rival the beauty and picturesque qualities of the Venetian Pool and Casino that opened in 1924. Much later, after the bankruptcy of the Coral Gables Corporation and during the worst years of the nationwide depression, the City of Coral Gables would have two outstanding facilities built by the Works Progress Administration and the Civilian Conservation Corps, Fairchild Tropical Garden and Matheson Hammock.

2 1923

2 1926

recognized an opportunity to create a picturesque themed swimming pool. In fact the pool is so naturalistic with its rock outcroppings that create caves, grottos, and diving platforms, that it seems as if there was no human intervention whatsoever in its creation. The pool has been in operation as a public swimming pool continuously, except for a brief period in 1987 when the City undertook a two million dollar restoration that included the provision of a handicapped lift, and a method to recycle the more than 800,000 gallons of water that it takes to fill the pool.

3
The Country Club of Coral Gables, 997 North Greenway Drive, 1923; Two-story Addition 1924, Hampton & Ehmann, Architects
The Country Club of Coral Gables was built in the heart of a residential area. Built of coral rock, the design featured an arcaded loggia overlooking the Granada Golf Course where diners could leisurely watch the play.

1
First Methodist Church, 536 Coral Way, 1933, Phineas Paist and Harold Steward, Architects
Paist and Steward were also the architects of the City Hall at 405 Biltmore Way. When a new church was completed in 1955, this building became the Parish Hall.

2
Venetian Pool and Casino, 2701 De Soto Boulevard, 1924, Denman Fink and Phineas Paist, Architects
The artist's vision for the Venetian Pool was to create an impression of the Old World charm of Venice transplanted into the lushness of the sub-tropics. The tile roof

towers frame a loggia that provides shelter and creates a spatial backdrop for the pool itself. The pool had its beginnings as a rock quarry from which the oolitic limestone was crushed to pave roadbeds and larger pieces used in the accent of houses. Rather than simply paving it over, the talented designers

3 4 1924

5 1925

Its three-stage tower was the focal point of the design and provided the main entry to the building. The Club was used as a place to entertain potential clients, and was so popular that a two-story addition was made the following year. The new wing housed dining rooms and a kitchen. Almost all of the original building was destroyed in a devastating fire in 1983. The tower however, was reconstructed and financed in part by a grant from the State of Florida.

4
The Granada 9 Hole Golf Course, 1923, Langford & Moreau (Chicago), Designers
The nine-hole, 58-acre Granada Golf Course lies between North and South Greenway Drives, directly adjacent to the Country Club. A few months before the course opened on January 1, 1923 landscape architect Frank Button observed that: "The nine-hole course is well underway now, and is 2,900 yards in length, with a 500 yard hole which will be a test for even the par golfers."

The course is still very popular today, and is a public course open to all.

5
The Alhambra Water Tower Intersection of Ferdinand Street, Alhambra Circle, and Greenway Court, 1924, Denman Fink, Designer
Built in 1924 as one of a pair of water towers designed to resemble lighthouses, the tower was used until 1931 when Coral Gables began getting its water from the City of Miami. The other tower located at Indian Mound Trail and Valencia Avenue was severely damaged in the hurricane of 1926 and was not rebuilt. The existing water tower on Alhambra was damaged over the years, but was completely restored by the City of Coral Gables in 1993 using vintage photographs to recreate some of the detail.

6
St. Phillips Episcopal Church and School, 1142 Coral Way, 1943, 1953, 1956
This beautiful church that is inspired by Tudor Revival architecture is of fairly recent construction, but its history is not. St. Phillips was founded in 1943 as a result of the gas rationing during the War that prevented many Episcopalian parishioners from attending St. Stephens, their church in Coconut Grove. The first service was held in an existing building (the first telephone exchange) and the next year, the remodeled and enlarged St. Phillips Church was opened. Over the years the parish has grown and its educational mission expanded. The complex now extends from Andalusia Avenue to Coral Way and Columbus Boulevard in a well-established residential area.

7
St. Teresa Catholic School, 2701 Indian Mound Trail, 1926, Walter DeGarmo, Architect
Originally named the Academy of St. Joseph, the school was built as a boarding school as well as a day school. The enrollment at that time included kindergarten through high school. Today the school is limited to those children in grades one through six.

8
Church of the Little Flower & Parish Hall, 1265 Anastasia Avenue, Parish Hall, 1927, Church, 1951, G. M. Barry and E.O. Kay, Architects
The growth of the Catholic community made the original church, built in 1927, obsolete. In response to the growing need, the original architects, still in practice, designed the 1951 church in a remarkably compatible way. The sanctuary of the new church is particularly beautiful, and Easter services have often been broadcast from here.

9 | 1925

9
Coral Gables Congregational Church, 3010 De Soto Boulevard, 1925, Richard Kiehnel, Architect

The first church to be built in Coral Gables, George Merrick donated the land in appreciation for his own faith, and for that of his late father, a Congregational minister. The church has retained both its superb exterior as well as its interior spaces that convey an intense spiritual experience through the combination of understated layering of paint, the use of exposed wooden trusses and ribs in the apse area, and the translucent art glass of the windows. Richard Kiehnel was one of the original six architects that were chosen to design the City of Coral Gables. His Pittsburgh firm (Kiehnel and Elliott) was chosen by Pittsburgh Steel President John Bindley to design his palatial estate, "El Jardin" in Coconut Grove in 1917 (now Carrolton School for Girls). Kiehnel was equally adept at residential, institutional, and commercial designs. Among his designs are the Seybold Building and the Scottish Rite Masonic Temple (in downtown Miami).

10
The Biltmore Hotel and Country Club, 1200 Anastasia Avenue, 1926, Schultze and Weaver (New York), Architects

In the grand plan for the city, nothing could be more important than its centerpiece, a resort hotel with luxurious accommodations and beautiful surroundings that would be unparalleled anywhere else. To achieve this paradigm of hospitality, Merrick turned to the most prominent hotelier in the country, John McEntee Bowman, the President of the Biltmore Hotel chain, who had already opened the New York Biltmore, The Havana Biltmore and the Atlanta Biltmore. Perhaps more than any, the Westchester Biltmore in Rye, New York was the model for the Coral

10 | Biltmore Hotel Club House drawing, 1924, Schultze & Weaver, Architects

10 1926

Gables hotel, as there, Bowman, a consummate sportsman, provided every possible outlet for the amateur athlete.

Bowman chose the New York firm of Leonard Schultze and S. Fullerton Weaver to design the hotel. The focal point of the composition was the central tower, modeled after the Giralda Tower from the Cathedral of Seville (Spain). The 15-story tower was set in the center of a 10-story block of the building that in turn was flanked by seven-story wings that extended out obliquely from the central mass.

Ground was broken in 1925, and the hotel became the center of the Riviera Section subdivision. The magnificent hotel and country club would turn its public face to Anastasia Avenue and the Coral Gables Congregational Church, and its leisure side to an enormous

36-hole golf course and a canal system that led to Tahiti Beach at Biscayne Bay and the ocean beyond.

The Miami-Biltmore Hotel opened to great fanfare in January 1926 at the height of the boom in Florida and with great optimism for its future. In fact, Merrick and Bowman were planning an even bigger, more stupendous version of the Biltmore Hotel in the soon to be developed Biscayne Section, south of Cocoplum (now Cartegena) Circle. However, less than eight months later, the end of the reckless optimism was in sight as a series of devastating events brought investors to their knees. On September 26, 1926 Miami was lashed with what would today be classified as a Category 4 hurricane that took hundreds of lives, and did damage estimated in the tens of millions. It was just the beginning.

Unsecured loans, the unavailability of building materials and the impending national financial disaster combined to end the extraordinary development envisioned for the City of Coral Gables.

Though it limped along with both Merrick and Bowman gone, the hotel never closed. And then, the unimaginable hapened. The United States went to war. In 1941, the Biltmore Hotel was pressed into service as an Army-Air Force Regional hospital. The glorious Biltmore Hotel, the most lavish and gracious of establishments was to be transformed. The needs of a hospital and those of a hotel were clearly at odds with one another. As a result, ceilings were dropped, fluorescent lights installed, linoleum replaced terrazzo, white wash covered the elaborate painted surfaces, the main lobby was partitioned to create a

10   1925

warren of offices and the enormous swimming pool, once the largest in the nation, was filled in and concreted over to provide sunning space for recuperating servicemen. The changes all but obliterated the incredibly rich original fabric of the building.

After the war, the hospital continued to operate under the Veterans Administration, until their new facility in downtown Miami opened in 1968. The Biltmore Hotel and Country Club was boarded and abandoned. It seemed that there was no other option than to demolish the grand hotel, as it had become an eyesore and liability to the city. Security and maintenance cost the city hundreds of thousands of dollars each year.

In 1972, the first in a series of events happened that shed some light on the possible positive outcome for restoring the Hotel. President Nixon passed the Legacy of Parks Act that allowed the government to give

surplus property to local governments, provided that there be a public recreational component. The City was awarded the property in a ceremony attended by Julie Nixon Eisenhower in April 1973.

Now that the City owned the property, the next question was how to use the buildings, and who would pay the costs (estimated in the multi-million dollar range). There were strong sentiments expressed by those who would save the buildings, and those who advocated their demolition.

By 1985, through a competitive selection process based on merit, a development firm was selected that would restore the building and bring it back to its original use. On January 1, 1987 after tens of millions were spent, the Hotel opened to an even greater fanfare than at its original opening. Although those first investors eventually encountered financial failure, a subsequent development team has insured the future of the Biltmore Hotel and Country Club for the

long term. There are a host of heroes in the long process that secured the future of the Hotel. The long history of the Biltmore Hotel is indeed a testament to all of the citizens of Coral Gables.

11
The Village at Merrick Park, 358 San Lorenzo Avenue, 2002, Spillis Candela & Partners, Architects 2002

The newest addition to Coral Gables' shopping experience is the recently completed Village at Merrick Park. The Village is a project of the Rouse Company, also the developers of the Bayside Market Place in downtown Miami. It is a very large mixed-use development in the traditional shopping center format with two major anchor stores, Neiman-Marcus and Nordstrom. The complex is constructed on 20 acres of city owned industrial land near the Dixie Highway and U.S. 1, which bisects Coral Gables. Its approval by the previous political administration was very controversial due to concerns over traffic and the impact it

11

would have on the existing business district approximately one mile away. The complex includes 435,000 square feet of high-end retailers and restaurants, and 110,000 square feet of class A office space. Under construction at this time is the Residences of Merrick Park, which will have 120 rental apartments and will be ready by fall of 2003. The architecture utilizes Mediterranean style motifs throughout, including the garages and the large pedestrian bridge spanning Ponce de Leon Boulevard.

12
Cartegena Circle (Cocoplum Circle) Intersection of Old Cutler Road, Sunset Drive, and Lejeune Road
The Circle marks the cut-off between the northern and originally developed plans for Coral Gables and the Biscayne Section, which was never completed. Old Cutler Road which leads south, was actually an early pioneer trail that led to the Village of Cutler, one of the earliest communities in Dade County formed in the 1880s. Cartegena Circle was originally named Cocoplum Circle, but was renamed to honor Coral Gables' Sister City of Cartegena Colombia. To the east is the subdivision named "Cocoplum," an exclusive residential community of multi-million dollar homes.

13
Old Cutler Road
The drive along Old Cutler Road is a drive that is reminiscent of Old Florida, and is a magnificent canopied roadway. The road follows what had been little more than a cart path that led early pioneers through the dense hammocks. A great deal of the original coral rock walls are still in place, although much of housing is now high-end single family residences.

14
Matheson Hammock
Matheson Hammock is the second and only surviving beach facility in Coral Gables. It was the first public beach dedicated to the people of Dade County. Donated by William Matheson in 1930, the original 84 acres has been expanded to cover a total of 520 acres. In 1936 the Civilian Conservation Corps (CCC), one of the agencies authorized by the New Deal's Economic Recovery Act, began work at Matheson Hammock. They dredged the swimming lagoon, quarried the native coral rock and built the bath house, concession building, and bridges, Although seriously damaged by hurricanes in 1945 and 1965, Matheson Hammock is today a favorite in the itineraries of tourists who visit Miami-Dade County.

15
Fairchild Tropical Garden, Old Cutler Road, Dedicated in 1938

Colonel Robert Montgomery donated 58 acres of land for the creation of the garden. Named for David Fairchild, an internationally known and traveled botanist, the garden contains more tropical plants than in any other place in the mainland United States. Fairchild went on to become the creator and first director of the U.S. Department of Agriculture. The gardens were designed by landscape architect William Lyman Phillips, who directed the Civilian Conservation Corps in the creation of the Garden.

16
Pinewood Cemetery, Sunset Road and Erwin Road (SW 47th Avenue)

The pioneers of Dade County were limited in the places in which to inter the dead. Pinewood Cemetery is the second oldest in the county after the Miami City Cemetery. This sacred site is a local historic landmark in the City of Coral Gables,

and is administered by an Advisory Board appointed by the City Commission. There are few surviving monuments to the dead, but they include tributes to some of the county's earliest pioneers. Pinewood Cemetery is today a serene and beautiful tropical hammock that invites the visitor to a contemplative walk through history.

17
Temple Judea Synagogue, 5500 Granada Boulevard, 1967, Morris Lapidus, Architect

Temple Judea in Coral Gables is an exemplary work by noted Miami Beach architect Morris Lapidus who is best known for his fanciful tourist hotels; the famous Fontainebleau, the Eden Roc (recently restored), and the Americana (now Sheraton Bal Harbour). He was also an accomplished designer of synagogues. In Temple Judea, the front entrance elevation facing the South Dixie Highway is characterized by three bold,

flat-topped concrete shell arches filled with glass that illuminate the vestibule.

18
Ponce De Leon High School, 1000 Augusto Avenue, 1925, H. George Fink, Architect

This was the second public school to be built in Coral Gables (the first was Coral Gables Elementary on Ponce de Leon Boulevard). Called "University High School" in the original plans, the building was designed as one of nine that would cluster around a commons. The first three buildings, administration, home economics, and gymnasium were completed in 1925. As this new school was then located away from the center of the completed residential sections of Coral Gables, the streetcar line was extended south on Ponce de Leon to transport the children directly to the new school. When a new high school was built at LeJeune and Bird Roads in 1950, the former high school

18 1926

Mosaic, Casa Loma Hotel (demolished)

AUTHOR BRIEFS

Aristides J. Millas has been an associate professor at the University of Miami School of Architecture since 1974, teaching design and history. He holds a bachelor's degree of Architecture from Carnegie Mellon University (1958) and a master's degree of Architecture in Urban Design from Harvard University (1964). His professional experience in architecture and planning includes the design of new towns, many inner city revitalization projects and historic districts, two university master plans and related facilities, sports stadiums, Greek Orthodox churches, and other works located in Florida, Pennsylvania, New Jersey, Arizona, Athens, Greece, and elsewhere. Locally he has served on the boards of the Miami Design Preservation League and the Dade Heritage Trust. In Coral Gables he co-authored a city sponsored, award winning Central Business District study (1984), has served on the "Miracle Mile" task force and as historian to the Board of Architects (1993–1999). Since 1986 Professor Millas has developed and taught "The Architectural History of South Florida" with university sponsored research resulting in numerous publications, public seminars, workshops, presentations, and tours focusing on local history and development issues. His research contributed to the national designation of the Miami Beach Historic District on which he co-authored and edited *Old Miami Beach: A Case Study in Historic Preservation* which received an outstanding preservation media award from the Florida Trust (1995). Most recently he was the recipient of the Historic Preservation Award from the Miami Chapter of the American Institute of Architects.

Ellen J. Uguccioni joined the staff of the City of Coral Gables' Historic Preservation Division in 1986 and was promoted to director after the creation of a city department in 1994. She received her master's degree in Art and Architectural History from the University of Missouri at Kansas City in 1972. She is the author of *The Fountains of Kansas City, A History and Love Affair* (with Sherry Piland, 1985); *Coral Gables in Postcards, Scenes from Florida's Yesterday* (with Sam La Roue, 1988); and *The Biltmore Hotel, The Legacy Endures* (with Sam La Roue, 2002). Ms. Uguccioni has also written and lectured extensively about historic preservation to local, state, and national audiences. She served three terms on the Florida National Register Review Board as the architectural historian member. Among many awards, she received distinguished service awards from the Florida Trust for Historic Preservation and the Villagers, Inc. She is currently a member of the Florida Historical Commission, a Trustee of the Florida Trust for Historic Preservation, and a Trustee of the Historical Museum of South Florida.

SELECTED BIBLIOGRAPHY

Books

Ballinger, Kenneth. *Miami Millions: The Dance of the Dollars in the Great Florida Land Boom of 1925*. Miami: Franklin Press, 1936.

Beach, Rex. *The Miracle of Coral Gables*. New York: Currier and Hartford, 1926.

Behar, Roberto, and Maurice Culot, Editors. *Coral Gables An American Garden City*. Paris, France: Norma Editions, 1997.

Harner, Charles E. *Florida's Promoters: The Men Who Made it Big.* Tampa: Glade House, 1949.

Hollingsworth, Tracy. *History of Dade County, Florida*. Coral Gables: The Parker Art and Printing Assoc, 1949.

La Roue, Samuel D., and Ellen J. Uguccioni, *The Biltmore Hotel An Enduring Legacy*. Miami: Arva Parks & Co. and Centennial Press, 2002.

Merrick, George E. *Song of the Wind on a Southern Shore.* Boston: Four Seasons, 1920.

Ormond, Mark et al. *The Biltmore Revisited*. Miami: Metropolitan Museum and Art Center, 1981.

Parks, Arva Moore. *The Pathway to Greatness: Building the University of Miami.* Coral Gables: Lowe Art Museum catalog, 2002.

Standiford, Les. *Coral Gables: The City Beautiful Story*. Atlanta: Coral Gables Chamber of Commerce and Riverbend Books, 1998.

Weigall, Theyre Hamilton. *Boom in Florida*. London: John Lane, 1931 (also published as *Boom in Paradise*. New York: A. H. King, 1932).

Publications And Articles

Avenue Obispo, Coral Gables. Coral Gables: Parker Art Printing Assoc., 1924.

Button, Frank M. "Landscaping in Southern Florida." *Southern Architect and Building News* (1926):41.

"Coral Gables Homes of Many Types." *The Miami Herald*, 2-1-1927.

Coral Gables Cottage Homeowner's Guide. Coral Gables: City of Coral Gables Historic Preservation Division, 1993.

"Coral Gables Goes Forward." *Progress: Coral Gables*. Coral Gables: Parker Art Printing, 1926.

Coral Gables Today: The Miami Riviera. Coral Gables Corporation, 11-15-1926.

Douglas, Marjory Stoneman. *Coral Gables: Miami Riviera*. Coral Gables: Parker Art Publishing Co., 1-7-1927.

Freeland, Helen C. "George E. Merrick." *Tequesta Magazine* 1, no.14 (1942) Miami: South Florida Historical Assoc.

"Interview with George E. Merrick." *New York Times*. 3-15-1925.

SELECTED BIBLIOGRAPHY

"Interview with George E. Merrick." *Jacksonville Times Union*. 1-28-1925.

LaRoue, Samuel D., and Ellen J. Uguccioni, *Coral Gables in Postcards*. Miami: Dade Heritage Trust, 1988.

Merrick, George E. *Coral Gables, Florida's Most Beautiful and Finest Developed Suburb at Miami*. Coral Gables: Parker Art Printing Assoc., 1923.

Miami Riviera, Second Annual Progress Week. Coral Gables: Coral Gables Corporation, 11-8-1927.

Millas, Aristides J., and Nicholas Patricios, *Coral Gables Central Business District Study*. Coral Gables, Planning and Zoning Board, 1984.

Newest Facts about Coral Gables, 2nd Ed. Coral Gables: Parker Art Printing Assoc., 4-1-1926.

Paist, Phineas E. "Stucco—Color." *National Builder Magazine*, October 1924.

Pictorial Guide of Coral Gables, Florida. Coral Gables: A. B. Willis and Co., Miami Publishing Co., 1927.

Preserving Our Past: A Guide to Historic Preservation in Coral Gables. Coral Gables: City of Coral Gables Historic Preservation Division, 1993.

Price, Charles Matlock. "The New Mediterranean Architecture of Florida." *House Beautiful*, 1925.

Price, Charles Matlock. "Coral Gables-Miami, A Story of Vision and Achievement." *Arts and Decoration*, 1925.

Thielen, Benedict. "Coral Gables Makes Good." *Holiday Magazine*, Nov. 1957.

"Where Tropic Trade Winds Blow: Coral Gables, the Ideal American City, created and founded by George E. Merrick, in the Tropics of Florida." *National Magazine: Mostly About People*, Oct. 1925.

Uguccioni, Ellen. *Mediterranean Architectural Style Guide*. City of Goral Gables Planning Dept., 1987.

Wilkins, Woodrow. "Coral Gables: 1920's New Town." *Historic Preservation*, 1978.

Wilkins, Woodrow. "The City of Coral Gables, Florida: An Historic New Town." Washington: National Park Service, *Historic American Building Survey #FLA-219*. 1971.